The Pastor as an Enabling and Equipping Disciple

By
Bishop E. Lynn Brown
Presiding Prelate of the
Ninth Episcopal District of the
Christian Methodist Episcopal Church

Library of Congress Catalog Card Number:93-078819
Printed in the United States of America

Printed by Universal Printers
Nashville, Tennessee

TABLE OF CONTENTS

PREFACE

When standing on the Mount of observation of our nation and peeping through the spiritual telescope for a panoramic view of the intricacies of (Christendom) one gets more than a bird's-eye view of dying, cold, empty churches, with tearless eyes and prayerless lips. One is tempted to ponder almost congruently with Ezekiel that there is a valley full of dry bones and rumor has it that they are dead— dead from the complexity of over institutionalization; dead from excessive political shenaniganism; dead from the neglect of pastoral care; dead from over assessments; dead from historical attitudinal problems; dead from post-ministerial interference; dead from mismanagement; dead from the lack of openness; dead from misunderstanding, disappointments, unkept promises, estrangement, broken relationships and dead from sin. Yes! dead from the lack of discipleship training. There are dry bones in the valley and rumor has it that they are dead.

Most of the leaders in our church know that spiritually we are a valley of dry bones and they have heard the rumor in every corner of this land that they are dead. Is this rumor true? Are there a few exceptions? What will we do about the rumor if it is true? Well one thing we know, something is wrong in some of our local churches and institutions that our general church sponsors.

A church should never be ashamed to take an introspection of itself; it should never be afraid to re-evaluate its ministry and structure. The CME Church is no exception because there are dry bones in the valley and rumor has it that they are dead! I do not think that the rumor is true about the bones being dead, but I do think that there are spiritually dry bones in the valley of Christian Methodism. And I do know that there are some dead churches in the valley of our beloved Zion, and there are some dying churches in the valley of our communion.

When you know you are in the valley of negative attitudes of pastors, presiding Elders, Bishops and lay persons, what do you do? To whom shall you go? Let us deal, first with what you should not do.

1. **We must not** start fighting with other bones in the valley. We must remember that no one cares if **dry bones** fight. No one cares if dry bones shoot, cut, curse, blame, frame, or blemish dry bones, because rumor has it that they are dead anyway. Therefore, dry bones become invisible to the White House, to the State House, to City Hall and even to our own house. These various entities are happy when bones interface harmfully with other bones. So the bottom line is that nobody cares what dry bones do to dry bones- clergy or lay-because rumor has it that they are dead.

2. **We must not** fail to recognize our existential situation in the life and witness of God's church. We will address a portion of this problem in our section on **The Historical Problem In Christian Methodism.** But here we just want to remind you to consider certain existential questions: Who are we?. What are we? Where did we come from? Where are we going? How do we get there? Is our problem basically a spiritual problem?

3. **Once we have discovered what our problem is, we must not** follow a do-nothing or band-aid continuum. We must not remain stale and stagnate, like a pond in a cow pasture- no fresh inlet and no fresh outlet. We must not fish in shallow water, we must launch out into the deep; we must become open, dynamic, progressive and aggressive for our God who is the giver, protector, preserver, author and finisher of our faith. We must, through the activities of the Holy Spirit, become divinely illumined to the breath of God- let God breathe on these dry bones, so that they may live. And the way to do this is to implement a sincere, strong and vigorous discipleship ministry in every local church. We must develop pastor who are enabling and equipping disciples in and of themselves. For Jesus said: "If you abide in my word you are my disciples indeed" (Luke 8:31).

This, in essence, is what the following pages are all about.

In this little book we want to make sure that the pastor knows what he/she is, who he/she is, whose he/she is and what it will take for him/her to become an **"Enabling and Equipping Disciple."**

Let me say at the outset that discipleship for the pastor or anyone else is not a supposed second step in Christianity , as if one first becomes a believer in Jesus before and after **"the Call and Ordination"** and then, if one chooses, becomes an enabling and equipping disciple. From the beginning, discipleship is involved in what it means to be a Christian pastor.

From a biblical perspective we hope the readers of the following pages will get more than a bird's-eye view of a road map that we believe will inevitably lead them into becoming more effective **Enabling and Equipping Disciples.**

This book is the result of the many constructive encounters I have had with various people across the nations as well as the experiences I have had as a pastor, General Officer and Presiding Bishop of the Ninth Episcopal District of the Christian Methodist Episcopal Church. Some of the material is a portion of the class I taught in the Sixth Convocation of our beloved Zion in Knoxville, Tennessee, 1992 and some thought from the Episcopal Address delivered at the 1990 General Conference.

I wish to thank my loyal secretary Miss Jean Thompson and my lovely devoted wife, Gladys, for typing the manuscript. Also I would like to thank the Rev. Paul A. Stewart, Sr., the effective pastor of Phillips Temple CME Church, Los Angeles, California, and Rev. Chester Tollette, the very efficient pastor of Calvary CME Church, Pasadena, California, Rev. James E. McGriff, Presiding Elder of the Oklahoma District, Oklahoma City, Oklahoma, Rev. Dr. Robert Peoples, pastor of Christ Temple in Tulsa, Oklahoma, Rev. Robert Holt, associate pastor, Phillips Temple, Los Angeles, California, Mrs. Esther Parks, Conference Treasurer for the Southern California

Conference and Vice President First Interstate Bank, Los Angeles, California, and Rev. Dr. Charles Belcher, pastor of Amos Temple, Los Angeles, California, for their many helpful suggestions and reading of the entire manuscript.

Finally, may I take this opportunity to thank all of the pastors, Presiding Elders, Bishops and wonderful lay persons with whom I have interfaced through the years that made this book possible. We may not be to able dispel the rumor, but we can, through the help of God, put flesh on the dry bones.

— E. Lynn Brown

INTRODUCTION

There is a critical need in the Christian Methodist Episcopal Church to make disciples.

At the center of the church, we are not only facing a crisis, but we are in the midst of a crisis. We are in the midst of a severe crisis because over 90%, in many instances, of the laity of the church are untrained, uninvolved and unfruitful in a meaningful way, in light of the Biblical metaphors denoting Christian disciples as salt, leaven, light, army, and ambassadors, which portrays our task and mission. We are to penetrate the world and make it better. One can easily observe that among most church members this is not happening.

This critical need to make disciples was echoed by Elton Trueblood. He writes:

> Perhaps the greatest single weakness of the contemporary Christian church is that millions of supposed members are not really involved at all and, what is worse, do not think it strange that they are not. As soon as we recognize Christ's intention to make His church a militant company we understand at once that the conventional arrangement cannot suffice. There is no real chance of victory in a campaign if ninety percent of the soldiers are untrained and uninvolved, but that is exactly where we stand now.

Based upon the accurate assertion of Dr. Trueblood, unless the church effectively deals with the problem of making disciples, the it does not have a chance of winning the battle of alleviating many of the social ills of our society nor of developing other disciples in significant numbers to assist in addressing these problems. Therefore, we stand at a very critical and dangerous point in the life of the church and something radical must be done in order to change the attitude and direction of its ministry.

James Montgomery Boise points out in his book,

Christ's Call To Discipleship, that there is a fatal defect in the life of Christ's church in the twentieth century: a lack of true discipleship. **Discipleship** means forsaking everything to follow Christ. But for many of today's supposed Christians- perhaps the majority - the case is that while there is much talk about Christ and even much more furious activity, there is actually very little following of Christ Himself. And that means in some circles there is very little genuine Christianity. Many who fervently call Him "Lord, Lord" are not Christians (Matthew 7:21) , whether they are in the pulpit or the pew.

We should not be surprised by this, because Jesus Himself said that this would be the case. But we should be distressed by it.

In Jesus' great sermon on the Mount of Olives, uttered shortly before His crucifixion, Jesus compared professing (but unconverted) Christians to women waiting for a bridegroom to appear for a wedding banquet. They were unprepared for His coming and were therefore shut out of the wedding. They were not saved. Again, Jesus compared professing Christians to a man who was given a talent to invest but who failed to use it and was condemned by the master on the day of reckoning. Jesus said that he was thrown "into the darkness, where there will be weeping and gnashing of teeth" (Matthew 25:30). In a third comparison He described these people as failing to feed the hungry, give drinks to those thirsting, receive strangers, clothe the naked, care for the sick, and visit those who were imprisoned.

These people called Jesus "Lord." They considered themselves to be genuinely converted persons, but they were not Christians and so perished.

We need to see where this is true in our churches. We need to ask what it means to be a Christian and whether those shortcomings are descriptions of ourselves.

There are several reasons that this concept is common in today's church. The first is a defective theology that has crept over us like a deadening fog. This theology separates faith from discipleship and grace from obedience. It teaches that Jesus can be received as one's Savior without being received as one's Lord. This is why I always greet people in the name of Him who is our Redeemer, Savior and Lord! Many people want Christ to be their Redeemer and Saviour but not their Lord. Our spiritual journey is not a cafeteria line where we can choose what we want and leave the rest. It is all or none.

This is a common defect in times of prosperity. In the days of hardship, particularly persecution, those who are in the process of becoming Christians count the cost of discipleship carefully before taking up the cross of the Nazarene. Preachers do not beguile them with false promises of an easy life or indulgence of sins. But in good and prosperous times the cost does not seem so high, and people take the name of Christ without undergoing the radical transformation of life that true conversion implies. In these times, preachers often delude them with an "easy" faith - Christianity without the cross - in order to increase the numbers on their church rolls, whether or not the added people are regenerated and renewed.

Dietrich Bonhoeffer, the German churchman of the Nazi era who eventually suffered martyrdom for his opposition to Hitler's policies, called this erroneous theology "cheap grace." He said in his book, *The Cost of Discipleship*,

> "Cheap Grace is the preaching of forgiveness without requiring repentance, baptism without church discipline, communion without confession, absolution without personal confession. Cheap grace is grace without discipleship, grace without the cross, grace without Jesus Christ living and incarnate."

The contrast is "costly grace." Bonhoeffer reminds us that

> **costly grace is the treasure hidden in the field; for the sake of it a man will gladly go and sell all that he has. It is the pearl of great price, to buy which the merchant will sell all his goods. It is the kingly rule of Christ, for whose sake a man will pluck out the eye which cause him to**

> stumble; it is the call of Jesus Christ at
> which the disciple leaves his nets and fol-
> lows him. Costly grace is the gospel which
> must be sought again and again, the gift
> which must be asked for, the door at
> which a man must knock. Such grace is
> costly because it calls us to follow, and it
> is grace because it calls us to follow Jesus.

Another writer, an American, bemoaned the same situation. Chicago pastor and devotional author A. W. Tozer declared:

> The doctrine of justification by faith - a Biblical truth and a blessed relief from sterile legalism and unavailing self-effort - has in our time fallen into evil company and been interpreted by many in such manner as actually to bar men from the knowledge of God. The whole transaction of religious conversion has been made mechanical and spiritless. Faith may now be exercised without a jar to the moral life and without embarrassment to the Adamic ego.

Christ may be "received" without creating any special love for him in the soul of the receiver. The person is "saved," but he/she does not hunger or thirst after God. In fact he/she is specifically taught to be satisfied and encouraged to be content with little.

It is a false theology that has encouraged this fatal lack of discipleship. The error is also due to the absence of what the older devotional writers called a "self-examined life."

Most Westerners live in a tragically mindless environment. Life is too fast, and our contact with other persons too impersonal for any real thought or reflection. Even in the church we are far more often encouraged to join this committee, back this project, or serve on this board than we are counseled to examine our relationship to God and His Son Jesus Christ. So long as we are performing for the church, few question whether our profession is genuine or spurious. But sermons should suggest that members of a church may not actually be saved, although they are members. Teachers should stress that a personal, self-denying, costly, and persistent following of Christ is necessary if a person is to be acknowledged by Jesus at the final day. This is the best way to dispel the rumor and put flesh on the bones.

In the absence of this teaching millions drift on, assuming that because they have made verbal acknowledgment of Christ ten, twenty, or even thirty years ago and have done nothing terribly bad since, they are Christians, when actually they may be far from Christ, devoid of grace, and in danger of perishing forever. Yes! The bones are dry but it is nothing that true discipleship can not cure, in spite of the fact that rumor has it that they are dead.

The making of Christian disciples is the call of the hour, as it has been the call of every hour when Jesus has been taken seriously. And when the call does come, it comes as a challenge and as a compulsion. This challenge becomes more compelling as we come to grips with the fact that making disciples is not only optional service for Christians, but we must make disciples in order to be Christians.

Chapter 1
The Meaning of Christian Discipleship

DISCIPLE WAS CHRIST'S favorite word for those whose lives were intricately linked with his. The Greek word for disciple, **mathetes** is used *269 times* in the Gospels and Acts. It means a "taught" or "trained" one.

In the Gospel of John, Jesus defines the word **disciple** in three ways.

First, a disciple is a Christian who is involved in the word of God on a continual basis. "Then said Jesus to those Jews which believed on him, If ye continue in my word, then are ye my disciples indeed" **(John 8:31)**. *The Bible* is much more than a mere book; *it is a reliable guide for daily living.* The continual application of Scripture results in learning the truths which, according to Jesus, set one free **(see John 8:32)**.

Second, a disciple is one *who lays down his life for others.* "A new commandment I give unto you, that ye love one another; as I have loved you, that ye also love one another. By this shall all men know that ye are my disciples, if ye have love one to another" **(John 13:34-35)**.

But what kind of love is this? Is it far more than merely doing a few good deeds. In **John 15:13**, Jesus says, "Greater love hath no man than this, that a man lay down his life for his friends." This gives love a far deeper meaning: a disciple loves enough to be unpopular, to be misunderstood, to stand alone, to suffer. Love is unconditional.

Third, a disciple is one who abides daily in a fruit-bearing *union with Christ.* Jesus said:

Abide in me, and I in you, As the branch cannot bear fruit of itself, except it abide in the vine; no more can ye, except ye abide in me. I am the vine, ye are the branches: He that abideth in me, and I in him, the same bringeth forth much fruit: "for without me ye can do nothing" **(John 15:4-5).**

The word "fruit" is used several ways in the Scriptures. This passage seems to be more illustrative of the fruit of our union with Christ, rather than the fruit of the Spirit as explained in **Galatians 5:22-23.** This is further discussed in John 15:8: "Herein is my Father glorified, that ye bear much fruit; so shall ye be my disciples."

So Christ's disciples are those who bear fruit that comes from abiding in union with Him. Christ's prayer for the disciples recorded in John 17 shows that the fruit mentioned in John 15 is people: "Neither pray I for these alone, but for them also which shall believe on me through their word" (John 17:20).

> **A disciple is a Christian who is growing in conformity to Christ, is achieving fruit in evangelism, and is working in follow-up to conserve his fruit.**

James M. Boise does an excellent job in describing the Elements of Discipleship. They are:

1. **Obedience.** Obedience is an unpopular concept today betrayed by our frequent use of the phrase "blind obedience," meaning mindless adherence to authority. We think of it as enemy soldiers blindly carrying out the inhuman orders of an evil commander. So when we come to a phrase like "follow me" we naturally think of it as an invitation and conform our evangelism to that pattern. We "invite" people to follow Jesus, promising that He will receive them and make them happy. Well, there may be an element of invitation in Christ's call to sinners, but the words "follow me" are in the imperative mood and are therefore a command — which is why those commanded to follow Jesus did in fact immediately leave their nets, boats, counting tables, or whatever else was occupying them and followed Jesus. On His lips the command "Follow me" was no more resistible than the command to Lazarus to "come out" **(John 11:43).** It was the equivalent of what theologians term God's "effective call."

That is another way of saying that without obedience there is no real Christianity. It is not that people cannot "follow" Jesus in a lesser sense and then fall away when the demands of genuine discipleship become clear to them. Many persons in the gospels seem to have done this. The rich young ruler is an example. But that is not the same as a sheep of Christ's flock hearing His call and responding to His voice as he recognizes Jesus as his Lord and Master. Those who are genuinely Christ's sheep obey His call from the beginning and enter into a life characterized by obedience.

2. **Repentance.** When Jesus called Matthew, He called one who was a recognized sinner. So He emphasized repentance: "I have not come to call the righteous, but sinners to repentance" **(Luke 5:32).** But the need for repentance is no less evident in the calls of the other disciples. For example, in both Matthew and Mark the account of the calling of the first disciples is immediately preceded by a record of Christ's first preaching, focusing on the words "repent, for the kingdom of heaven is near" **(Matthew 4:17; cf. Mark 1:14).** In Luke's account the equivalent story is embedded in Jesus' first miraculous intervention in the disciples' fishing, where they caught so many fish the net was breaking. That story records Peter's profound experience of Christ's holiness and of his own sin that led him to cry out, "Go away from me, Lord; I am a sinful man!" **(Luke 5:8).** The point is that it is impossible to follow Christ without repentance.

How could it be otherwise? Jesus is the holy, sinless Son of God. He has never taken one step in any sinful direction. he has never been led by the way into a single sinful thought. So anyone who is following Him is not following some imaginary Jesus. Therefore he/she must by definition turn his/her back away from sin and set his/her face toward righteousness. Yet, Christians do sin. When they do they must confess it and turn from it, in order to become restored to fellowship again. And anyone who thinks he can follow Christ without renouncing sin is dreadfully confused. Moreover, anyone who claims to be following Christ while actually continuing in unrighteousness is deluded; and he or she is not a Christian.

3. **Submission.** In one of Jesus' most important sayings about discipleship, which we will study more carefully in the next chapter, the Lord pictures discipleship as putting

on a yoke. This suggests a number of things, but chiefly it suggests submission to Christ for His assigned work. It is the picture of an animal yoked to others as well as to a plow.

A yoke is also the connection between submission and subjection. "Submit" comes from the two Latin words "sub" (meaning "under") and "mitto," "mittere" (meaning "to put" or "place"). So submission means putting oneself under the authority of another. "Subject" also comes from two Latin words, in this case "sub" (meaning "under") and "iacto", "iactare" (meaning "cast" or "throw"). It means being put under the authority of another. In other words, although the first word has an active sense (I put myself under another's authority) and the second word has a passive sense (I am placed under that authority), the idea is nevertheless essentially the same. The root meanings of both words are connected with "yoke" in this way. In ancient times it was customary for a ruler, when he had conquered a new people or territory, to place a staff across two upright poles, perhaps four feet off the ground, and the require the captured people to pass under it. By this act they passed under his yoke or submitted to his authority. When Jesus used this image He was saying that to follow Him was to submit to Him. It was to receive Him as Lord of one's life.

4. **Commitment.** The fourth element, commitment,is vital for the simple reason that it is impossible to follow Christ without being committed to Him. A lack of commitment means deviating from His path or falling away from Him. On the other hand, it is impossible to be committed to Christ without following Him, for a failure to follow really means being committed to some other thing or person.

Surprisingly, this has become a hotly contested issue today on grounds that teaching commitment to Christ is to add something else to faith, which is a false gospel. This is the view, for example, of Charles C. Ryrie, former dean of doctoral studies and professor of systematic theology at Dallas Theological Seminary. He writes,

> The message of faith only and the message of faith plus commitment of life cannot both be the gospel; therefore, one of them is a false gospel and comes under the curse of perverting the gospel or

preaching another gospel **(Galatians 1:6-9).**

Those who hold to this position do not deny that commitment is a good thing in and of itself or that is necessary for growth in the Christian life. But they do deny that commitment stands at the beginning in the sense that one cannot really be saved without it. They would even take issue with a lordship of Christ expressed as **"willingness to commit one's life absolutely"** to Him, the implication being that it is possible to believe on Jesus as one's Savior from sin without willingness to follow Him.

Three arguments are advanced in support of the above line of thought. First, Scripture contains examples of believers who were not completely committed to Jesus and yet were saved. Peter resisted Christ's authority **(Acts 10:14).** Barnabas disagreed with Paul over whether they should take John Mark along with them on a second missionary journey **(Acts 15:39)**. Certain believers at Ephesus apparently refused to give up their magic charms and books for as long as two years after they had become a Christian **(Acts 19).** Lot was saved and was declared a righteous man by God even when he was living in Sodom **(II Peter 2:7-8).**

The issue, however, is not whether believers sin, obviously, they do. It is whether they can come to Christ in faith while at the same time denying or resisting His lordship over them. This is that which is impossible.

A second argument is based on the meaning of the word "Lord." It is reasoned that in reference to Jesus, Lord means "God Jesus" or "Jehovah Jesus." According to this view since Lord mean "Jehovah," all other meanings are excluded. Consequently, "Lord" does not mean "Master." But "Lord" does mean "Master". That is why a word that was originally used on the human level to denote one who is sovereign over slaves is also used of God.

Jehovah is called Lord because He is Master. He is the sovereign Master, hence, the *Kyrios* of which all other *kyrioi* are but shadows. Who is God if He is not Master? If God is not sovereign, He is not God. No other God than the sovereign God is presented to us in the Bible.

A third argument is the one suggested earlier, namely, that to insist on the lordship of Christ in salvation is to require something other than the work of Christ. It is to add works to faith, which is as all true Christians confess, a false gospel. Dr. Ryrie seems to have this in mind as he concludes, "If you are ever tempted to add something to the uncomplicated grace of God, first try making it crystal clear who is the Object of faith and what is its content. Then point men to Him, The Lord Jesus, the God-Man Saviour, who offers eternal forgiveness to all who believe."

Yet, this is precisely the point on which all true believers insist. We do not wish to add anything to Christ's finished work; it is for that very reason that we direct believers to the Lord Jesus Christ. But He is the Lord Christ. This Lord is the object of faith and its content. There is no other. Consequently, if faith is directed to one who is not Lord, it is directed to one who is a false Christ of the imagination. Such a one is not the Savior, and He will save no one.

Moreover, there is the meaning of faith itself, is "faith" minus commitment a true biblical faith? We remember that the apostle James goes so far as to insist — in a passage some have erroneously thought contradicts the Pauline doctrine of justification by faith — that faith without works is dead **(James 2:17,26)**. Such "faith" is useless (v.20) and worth nothing (v. 16). It is a claim to faith only (v. 14) and not a genuine faith which comes of God and expresses itself in works that pleases Him. But if that is true — if faith without works is dead — how much truer it is that faith without commitment is also dead. True faith involves these elements: **knowledge,** upon which it is based; **heart response,** which results from the new birth; and **commitment,** without which "faith" is no different from the assent of the demons who "believe... and shudder" **(James 2:19).** No one is saved by a dead faith. But a living faith is faith in Jesus as Lord and Savior, for the Lord is the Savior and the Savior is the Lord.

One must be appreciative of the concern of Dr. Ryrie and those who think like him in preserving the purity of the gospel. We agree wholeheartedly that any addition to the perfect work of Christ by sinful men and women perverts the gospel and is destructive to Christianity. If works enter into salvation in any way, those who trust in them are not saved by Jesus and are lost. All true Christians agree in that. But any attempt to divorce Christ as Savior from Christ as Lord also perverts the gospel, for anyone who believes in a Savior who is not the Lord is not believing in the true Christ and is not regenerate.

5. **Perseverance.** The final important element in the following of Christ is perseverance. This is because following is not an isolated act, done once and never to be repeated. It is a lifetime commitment that is not fulfilled here until the final barrier is crossed, the crown received, and it and all other rewards laid gratefully at the feet of Jesus.

Is salvation something that takes place in the past, something that is taking place now, or something that is to take place at the Lord's return? The answer is that all three are salvation and that isolating any one is an error fatal to the preservation of the gospel. Salvation took place in the past. So it is right to say that Jesus saved us by His death on the cross. His death redeemed His people. His blood made atonement for their sins. But this is not the only way the Bible speaks of salvation. It also speaks of a present element, of our "being saved" **(I Corinthians 1:18).** Moreover, it looks forward to a time when by the continuing grace of God we will be saved utterly. With that blessed end in view it admonishes us to persevere in our commitment. Jesus said, "All men will hate you because of me, but he who stands firm to the end will be saved" **(Matthew 10:22).** Peter spoke of growth in godliness and concluded:

> Therefore, my brothers, be all the more eager to make your calling and election sure. For if you do these things, you will never fall, and you will receive a rich welcome into the eternal kingdom of our Lord and Savior Jesus Christ" **(II Peter 1:10-11).** Paul said, "Work out your salvation with fear and trembling, for it is God who works in you to will and to act according to his good purpose **(Philippians 2:12b-13).**

All this is to say that discipleship is not simply a door to be entered but a path to be followed and that the disciple proves the validity of his discipleship by following that path to the very end. David wrote about it in Psalm 119. The section that begins, "Your word is a lamp at my feet and light for my path," ends with, "My heart is set on keeping your decrees to the very end"   (Psalm 119: 105,112). That is it! The true disciple follows Jesus to the end of everything.

In the last years of the seventeenth century a French aristocrat wrote a book on discipleship that became a classic in the field. At one time the book was publicly burned in France. Yet it has been received by millions who have judged it one of the most helpful books ever written. It was loved by Fenelon, Count Zinzendorf, John Wesley, and Hudson Taylor. This aristocrat was Madame Jeanne Guyon. Her book bears the title Experiencing the Depths of Jesus Christ (French title: Le Moyen Court et Tres Facile de Faire Oraison). As she wrote this classic, Madame Guyon had a high standard of discipleship in view, but at the same time she was aware that the call to follow Christ was not some circumscribed invitation to be delivered only to a special body of believers or to all believers only as a second step in their religious experience. On the contrary, it is the essence of faith, and the invitation to come to Christ as a disciple for all. She wrote:

> If you are thirsty, come to the living waters. Do not waste your precious time digging wells that have no water in them. ...If you are starving and can find nothing to satisfy your hunger, then come. Come, and you will be filled.
>
> You who are poor, come.
>
> You who are afflicted, come.
>
> You who are weighted down with your load of wretchedness and your load of pain, come. You will be comforted!
>
> You who are sick and need a physician, come. Don't hesitate because you have diseases. Come to your Lord and show him all your diseases, and they will be healed! Come.

This is the invitation that Christ's call to discipleship holds for every person. To be a Christian is no light matter. It is a call to a transformed life and to perseverance through whatever troubles may arise. It may be the hardest thing anyone can do. Yet anyone can do it, with Christ supplying the necessary strength. In the end it is the only thing that really matters. Will you take that path?

The Master is going before you. He is looking back at you with a most compelling gaze. He is saying, "COME!" He is commanding, "follow me!"

Chapter 2
The Historical Problem in Christian Methodism

You and I are cognizant of the fact that there is not a denomination or communion anywhere that has contributed more to humankind, proportionally, than the Christian Methodist Episcopal Church. In the areas of education, race relations, ecumenism, social out-reach ministries, church politics and assessments, we take a back seat to no Christian communion. But what about the Biblical mandate of Discipleship Ministry? How have we fared in this essential Christian arena?

I personally feel that the major historical problem of Christian Methodism has been in the area of Christian Discipleship. If our great beloved Zion is going to grow numerically spiritually and financially, we are going to have to recapture the imperative of discipleship ministry. There must be a refocusing of our total ministry. Bishop Richard B. Wilkes points out in his book, *And Are We Yet Alive?* that "we may be looking through a pair of binoculars that are out of focus." That is to say, we may not be seeing clearly. Our attention today just may be directed elsewhere. Please allow me ask a few questions. Do the essentials go undone? Are we almost, always, too nearsighted? If so, has this nearsightedness made us a church turned inward? Do we spend too much time oiling the wheels of our organizational structure? Originally, we were called Methodists because we had a plan, a *viable dynamic organization,* a workable and effective people—oriented method. Does our methodology work effectively in a technocratic society? Does our organizational genius consume and subsume our most promising talent? Has our structure become an end in and of itself? Are our worship services too dull and dry? Do we need alternatives to our present worship services? What are we going to do about our dying rural churches? Do we really know who we are technologically? Do we have a data bank in this computerized age, such as, what percentage of the nation's population are we? What percentage of the black population are we? What percentage of us are female, male, teenagers, senior citizens, retired and living on a pension and social security? How many single parent households are headed by a male or female? What percent of our membership are renters, homeowners, or landlords? What percentage of our families live below the poverty level? What is the average age in our churches? What is the average income of our church? Are we growing numerically, spiritually, morally, and financially? If so, why? If not, why not? Yes! we have been around for one hundred twenty two years; and we have accomplished many marvelous things. But, what about today? Are we ready for the nineties? Are we ready for the twenty-first century? We do know, however, that in some churches the Commission on Evangelism meets, but does not make any calls. The social concerns phase of the commission gather, but does not write any letters or do any community outreach. The educational leaders complain about Scripture illiteracy but do not read the Bible. The church conference assembles to hear reports from auxiliaries, adopt resolutions from various persons, and approve budgets, but no one is discipled. Everybody goes home tired, thinking that they've done the work of the church.

John and Charles Wesley encountered some of the same problems. They rejected organizational complexity. In Bristol, on the first of August in 1745, in the "New Room", the two brothers met with nine other preachers. The names of fourteen assistants were read, and a new rule was added to the twelve they had adopted the year before. It read, "You have nothing to do but save souls; therefore, spend and be spent in this work. And go always, not to those who need you, but to those who need you most." The fathers of our great Zion did not get bogged down in organizational complexity. *Miles, Vanderhorst, Holsey, Beebe* and *Lane* went to those who needed them, and to those who needed them most. They walked across the cornfields of Tennessee, the cotton fields of Georgia, the sugarcane fields of Louisiana, the rice fields of Arkansas, the fertile crescents of Texas, the deltas of Mississippi, and the blue grass of Kentucky, saving souls. They were in focus; they saw clearly. It was a church turned outward and it grew in leaps and bounds. We must refocus the ministry of our great Zion.

When any Institution reaches the point and time in its history when it serves itself, its spiritual immune system becomes deficient and can no longer resist the deadly germ of stagnation. Therefore, it contracts the terminal disease of ingrowness and dies. We must refocus our church. How can we do this ?

In order to refocus the spiritual binoculars of the CME Church, we must return the total ministry of our church to the authentic word of God. *As great as our men's and women's days are;* as glorious as our founder's days are; as precise as our commencement exercises are; as succinct as our plenary sessions are; as wonderful as our baccalaureates are; as beautiful as our missionary marches are; as impressive as our General Conferences, General Boards, Annual Conferences, District Conferences and local church services are; as talked about as our finances are; as articulate, profound, exegetical and structurally prepared our speeches and sermons have become they cannot substitute for the old fashioned Bible-centered, Spirit-filled church. The churches today that are winning souls to Christ, that are ministering effectively to the drug addicts, the drop outs, the foster homes, the alcoholics, the race track addicts, the aged, the incarcerated, the lost and spiritually bankrupted person, are the churches that have the Bible as their center piece; they are Bible-centered churches.

We must reaffirm the teaching, the preaching, and

the living of the sound unadulterated word of God.

We feel that most of the major problems in our society today are basically spiritual— a lack of sound Biblical doctrines and values in the home, church and community. We feel that even African Americans cannot justly blame all of our own ills on the white race. Granted, racism is raising its ugly head again. In many firms, we are still the last hired and the first fired; some would like to see the destruction of black men and black boys; poverty in the black arena is on the down-side, and many other discriminatory practices and other forms of injustices appear to be on the increase. But even these unfortunate and inhumane treatments do not justify the way blacks treat each other, their families, their churches, their related institutions and themselves. Too long as a race we have excused ourselves from our moral and spiritual duties and responsibilities. What makes us think that we can sin and live wicked and immoral lives, yet expect God to excuse us? Can we be so foolish as to believe that we can willfully and consistently break the moral laws and commandments of God and not be punished? When it comes to the matter of wrong-doing, God will compromise with no one — not even those who were once slaves. Moral deterioration from within has destroyed other races, nations and churches; thus we urge the CME Church to let the word become flesh in our daily lives before it destroys us. Have we forgotten that. "Righteousness exalteth a nation; but sin is a reproach to any people" **(Prov. 14:34)**?

The CME Church today stands at the crossroads of decision and destiny. Ours is an hour of battle, obligation and oppurtunity. We must refocus out ministries.God is saying:

> If my people, who are called by my name,
> shall humble themselves, and pray, and seek
> my face, and turn from their wicked ways;
> then I will hear from heaven, and will forgive
> their sin and heal their land **(II Chro. 7:14).**

What will happen when we refocus the Christian Methodist Episcopal Church and initiate and implement a connectional Bible-centered ministry?

I believe that if every minister and layperson would recapture the authentic ring of the Bible connectionally, God would indeed bless us, even beyond our wildest imagination. This is God's requirement of His church.

God requires His church to be "the salt of the earth". If the church refuses to be salt or seasoning, it is then good for nothing but to be cast out and trodden under the foot of men. **(Matt. 5:13)**

God requires His church to be righteous and His word affirms that "all unrighteousness is sin" **(I John 5:17)**. Our communities must change so that God has a remnant with whom He can identify. "If my people who are called by My name would humble themselves ...." **(II Chr. 7:14, Isa. 55:7)**

God requires His church to promulgate His word. (Isa. 40:8; 55:11). God's word should be first and foremost on the agenda of the institutional church. No disciplinary structure, no ritualistic behavior, nor social creed, nor church membership vows should take the place of the teaching and proclamation of the Word of God and the Gospel it expresses. **(John 1:1, 14:24, Phil. 2:16).**

God requires that His church possess and teach faith **(II Tim. 4:7; Luke 17:5; Rom. 1:17; 10:17; II Cor., 5:7; Eph. 4:13; Heb. 11:1,16): for without faith it is impossible to please Him. FAITH FOR TOUGH TIMES — FAITH FOR TOUGH TASKS — FAITH FOR TOUGH TEACHING.** And how can the Christian Methodist Episcopal Church please God? Permit us to suggest a few ways: (1) The CME Church must emphasize sound Bible teaching **(II Tim. 4:2-3).** Teaching involves imparting information from the Bible. It also requires the relevant explanation and application of Biblical truth to the contemporary world.

Even our most profound oratories from the pulpits of Christian Methodism have not succeeded in producing the birth and growth of a large number of Christian disciples in the CME Church. The Bible was written to teach people how to live and Jesus left explicit instructions for us in **Matthew 28:20.**

The CME Church must use the spiritual gifts given by Christ to His body **(Rom. 12:4-5, I Cor. 12).** According to I Corinthians 12, God has constructed the spiritual body similar to the human body. It is made up of many parts, and every part has a function to fulfill in order for the whole body to operate properly. If one part is dysfunctional, it makes it more difficult for the body to achieve its goals.

Every believer in the CME Church on all levels must be held accountable to serve the rest of the church family so that the gifts of the body can be enhanced and leaders developed.

If the CME Church is going to get its members involved in ministry and the using of their spiritual gifts, there must be opportunity for them to serve.

The CME Church must discipline its members. **(Matthew 28:19-20).** Prior to His ascension into heaven Jesus Christ gave His small circle of disciples one of the most important and profound commands of His earthly ministry. The effective fulfillment of this command would determine the success of growth of the Kingdom of God. This commandment is often referred to as the Great Commission. The focal point of the command is that the main goal is to make disciples. Gary W. Kuhne, in his book, *The dynamics of discipline being and producing spiritual leaders,* gives us a meaningful and accurate definition of a disciple: "A disciple is a Christian who is growing in conformity of Christ, is achieving fruit in evangelism, and is walking in follow up to conserve His fruit."

This is the type of person the CME Church is commanded to develop. *A discipled member is one who has a basic understanding* of his faith; who has regular devotional time; who is involved in good fellowship; and who is instructed in the word of God. A discipled member is also one who obeys and applies what God has commanded him through the Bible.

We must learn how to disciple the laity effectively. The next decade and the years to come will belong to lay

Christians and to the preacher who knows how to teach them. *The day of clericalism is gradually* fading away. Clericalism is the notion that the preacher does all the religious work. Pastors must multiply themselves by training others. We must invest in others 'as did our mentors. They must become preachers/trainers and we, as Bishops, must continue to be pastor/layperson trainers. The text for the next decade should be 2 Tim. 2:1-2: "As for you my son, be strong through the Grace that is ours in union with Christ Jesus. Take the teachings that you heard me proclaim in the presence of my witnesses and entrust them to reliable people who will be able to teach others."

The CME Church must move from programs to ministry **(Ephesians 4:11-13)**. The horrendous plight of humankind and African-Americans in particular demands Christian Methodism move beyond status quo programs that may not be connected to ministry. Ministry is defined here as an activity in which the needs of people are met by Christian Methodists in accordance with the Scripture. Every event must qualify as ministry if it is going to help us address the crisis with which we are faced.

The Bible never describes programs that are not connected to ministry. Unless a program serves our brothers and sisters in Christ in accordance with the commands of God, it is not Biblical **(read Acts 6).** Unless some Biblically based goal is being met by a program, it is not ministry. Ministry through believers, not simply programs, is the main solution to our problems.

The CME Church must move beyond tradition **(Colossians 2:8).** Christian Methodism has a tremendous heritage as has been well pointed out above. Our history is a story of collective hope and unified faith in diverse situations. But however great is our heritage, we need to ask two questions about every activity of the church: Is it Biblical? and is it effective for ministry?

The traditions of persons are not always the traditions of God. It is amazing that we get angry at people if they do not follow tradition, but do not get upset if they disobey the Word. **Colossians 2:8** warns us to beware of "man-made" traditions.

Let us hasten to say, however, that many "old time ways" are important, not only for nostalgic reasons and the senses they give our heritage and history, but because many times they can reflect a clear picture of God. The gospels and spirituals are a prime example of something extremely valuable from the past that should be retained. We should never compromise those things, new or old, which give us a better understanding of who God is and what God has done.

The CME Church must implement responsive and responsible Christian stewardship. Jesus spent a great portion of his earthly ministry teaching important and imperative lessons in stewardship. These included the parables, isolated incidents and specific references to God's ownership and man's management responsibilities.

God has called the Christian Methodist Episcopal Church to *responsible Christian stewardship:* and God awaits our response:

> 1. To know what it means to be stewards of the ministries.
> 2 To learn the nature of stewardship and to grow as a denomination in Christian Stewardship.
> 3. To become a tithing church in faith and in practice. We must learn the theological, psychological, and common sense basis for tithing—obedience, special blessing as an act of faith.

In other words, we must subscribe to a Biblical and consistent method of financing the work of the church not as a legal requirement but as a spiritual challenge to a higher level of stewardship in the body of Christ.

The Pastor

The word "pastor" translates the Greek word poimen, which comes from a root word meaning to protect. Basically it means "shepherd," one who tends herds or flocks **(Eph. 4:11)**. *This word is used eighteen times in the New Testament. Eight times it refers to a "shepherd" of sheep* **(Matt. 9:36; 25:32; Mark 6:34; Luke 2:8, 15,18,20 John 10:2)**. *Seven* times it is used *symbolically of Jesus* **(Matt. 26:31; Mark 14:27; John 10:11-12,14,16)**. *One time it refers to "our Lord Jesus,* that great shepherd of the sheep" **(Heb. 13:20)**. *Once* it speaks of Christ as "the Shepherd and Bishop of your souls" **(I Peter 2:25)**. The only time where **poimen** is translated "pastor," and the only time that "pastor" appears in the New Testament, is in **Ephesians 4:11**. *Pastor comes from* **pastores**, the Latin equivalent of the Greek **poimen.** However, the other New Testament equivalences of **poimen** shed light upon its usage in **Ephesians 4:11.**

It should be noted, that the verb form, **poimanino** is used *eleven times* in the New Testament. *Three times it is rendered "rule"* **(Rev. 2:27; 12:5; 19:15)**. One time is translated *"feeding cattle"* **(Luke 17:7)**, where it might just as well read "feeding sheep" **(cf. I Cor. 9:7)**. In **Revelation 7:17** it speaks of the *Lamb feeding his sheep.* Elsewhere, except **Jude 12**, it refers to a *spiritual shepherd feeding the flock* of Christ **(John 21:16; Acts 20:28; I Peter 5:2)**.

This ministry of shepherding was committed to the *elders* who were also **overseers (Acts 20:17,28)**. Paul says to the elders of the church in Ephesus,

"Take heed therefore unto yourselves, and to all the flock, over which the Holy Spirit hath made you overseers, to feed the church of God, which he hath purchased with his own blood **(Acts 20:28)**." Peter holds this view, The elders which are among you I exhort, who am also an elder, and a witness of the sufferings of Christ, and also a partaker of the glory that shall be revealed: Feed the flock of God which is among you, taking the oversight thereof, not by constraint, but willingly: not for filthy lucre, but of a ready mind; Neither as being lords over God's heritage, but being ensamples to the flock **(I Peter 5:1-3).**

In **Acts 20:17, 28** the three term "elder," is inclusive of both "bishop," and "pastor". Hence, we may conclude that the *pastor is an elder or overseer. His work involves tender care and watchful superintendence.*

The Greek word *for overseer in the New Testament* is **episcopos.** It is usually translated bishop. Its root meaning is overseer (epi, meaning over, and *skopeo*, meaning to look or watch).

The term bishop or overseer indicates the character of the work undertaken. *In the new Testament there were at least two bishops in every local church* **(Acts 14:23; 20:17; Phil. 1:1; Titus 1:5; James 5:14).** When the singular is used, the passage is describing what a bishop should be **(I Tim. 3:2; Titus 1:7).** *Christ is spoken of as the "bishop of our souls"* **(I Peter 2:25).** The word episkope is rendered "office" in **Acts 1:20.**

The pastor of a church is the spiritual leader and shepard. His *functions* are *executive* and *not legislative.* Christ is the only lawgiver. In fulfilling this office, the manner and spirit of the work are of supreme importance. Specifically, the functions of pastors in the New Testament were the *administration of discipline, the settlement of disputes among Christians, the conducting of public services, the administration of the ordinances, the supervision of charities and the general oversight of the community. Preaching* and *teaching* were also a part of his/her duties.

The Pastor's Calling

In Ephesians 4:8-11 Paul interprets **Psalm 68:18** to depict the risen Christ's triumphant return to heaven. Through the rejoicing host he rides, with conquered death in chains following behind his chariot. In such entries among the ancients, the conquering hero scattered gifts among the celebrating throngs. But Paul says that Christ "gave gifts," not to the heavenly hosts, but also to "men."

And he names these gifts as *apostles, prophets evangelist,* and *pastors* and *teachers.* These were not spiritual gifts bestowed upon various people **(I Cor. 12:28),** but persons occupying these offices who were to minister to the saints in their growth and service **(Eph. 4:11-16).** The word "give," **edoke,** implies that Christ had called these persons to serve in these various functions.

To what do they refer? *"Apostles"* were spiritual pioneers who planted the gospel in new areas. *"Prophets"* were those with the ability to preach the gospel with unusual power. In modern parlance they might correspond to evangelist. Both apostles and prophets were itinerants with *no one established place of* service. *"Evangelists,"* perhaps were assigned to given areas, but not to individual churches. They were more like district missionaries working with groups of churches. *"Pastors and teachers"* refer to one office, and one which was related to one local church. A teacher might not necessarily be a pastor. But all pastors must be "apt to teach" **(I Tim. 3:2).**

The Pastor's Divine Calling

It has been noted that these persons were called to fill specific offices of service. The Christian life itself is the result of one's response to a call from God. He calls men out of darkness into light, out of spiritual death into life **(cf. Matt. 11:28-29; John 6:44).** The initiative in a saving relation is with God, but the response to the call in the will of man is also involved.

Likewise, God extends a call for service to all Christians. The Great Commission itself was given to others along with "the eleven disciples" **(Matt. 28:16-20)**. It is quite evident that Christians generally understood that they were to be witnesses to the gospel, **(Acts 6:8ff; 8:4ff; 18:26)**. One of Satan's greatest triumphs over the people of Christ was when he led them to divide themselves into the "clergy" and the "laity". The result was the loss of a sense of responsibility on the part of the latter, as the former was regarded as divinely appointed dispensers of grace. During recent years there has been a wholesome effort to return to the New Testament concept that witnessing is every Christian's job.

However, in this as in so many other things, one extreme has been replaced by another. Hence, today the attitude is widespread that God calls all Christians on the same basis. This serves to diminish the idea of a divine call being given to certain Christians for specific spiritual services, as over against other honored and useful vocations. For instance, the call of men to be physicians, lawyers, merchants, teachers, farmers, or any other vocation is equated with that of the pastor. Certainly men and women should serve God in whatever may be their vocations. But this is not to say that God, in a special way, does not call certain men and women to leave the normal pursuits of life to be set apart for some definite place of spiritual leadership.

The word "gave" in **Ephesians 4:11** speaks to the contrary. **Acts 20:28** clearly indicates that Paul regarded the office of pastor as a definite appointment of the Holy Spirit. In his own case the apostle was quite certain of a divine call in that Christ had placed him in the ministry **(I Tim. 1:12)**. Furthermore, he implied separation from material pursuits for spiritual service as he declared the Biblical principle "even so hath the Lord ordained that they which preach the gospel should live of the gospel" **(I Cor. 9:14; cf. Num. 18:8-20; I Cor. 9:1-19)**. This provision made by the Lord is his recognition that he does call some men and women in a peculiar way and for a peculiar service.

Biblical history lends abundant support to this truth. In the Old Testament there are the calls of Moses **(Exod. 3:10)**, Samuel **(I Sam. 3)**, Isaiah **(6:9)**, and Jeremiah **(1:5)**. In the New Testament also there is clear evidence of a divine call. Saul of Tarsus received his call shortly after a dramatic conversion experience. Saul became "a chosen vessel unto me, to bear my name before the Gentiles, and kings, and the children of Israel" **(Acts 9:15)**. The apostles were first called into the Christian life **(John 1:39-51)**. At a later time they were called to leave their material pursuits to follow Jesus in a peculiar mission **(Matt. 4:18-22; 9:9; Mark 3:13-19)**. To the eleven Jesus said, "Ye have not chosen me, but I have chosen you and ordained (appointed) you, that ye should go and bring forth fruit" **(John 15:16)**. In **John 15:16** and **Acts 9:15** the words for "chosen" carry the meaning of a selection from among others, and in this sense from among other Christians.

Therefore, the Scriptures teach the fact of a devine call given by God to specific persons for specific purposes. This does not diminish the sanctity of any vocation dedicated to God's will. But it does enhance the calling of those who are chosen of God for services of a peculiarly spiritual nature.

In order for the spiritual winds to come and bring sinners and flesh upon the dry bones of Christian Methodism, we must be "true to the heavenly", as was Ezekiel, **(Ezekiel 37:13-14)** and prophesy:

"And ye shall know that I am the Lord, when I have opened your graves, O my people, and brought you up from your graves.

I will put My Spirit in you, and you shall live, and I will place you in your own land. Then you shall know that I, the Lord, have spoken it and performed it, says the Lord."

And the thing you have heard me say in the presence of many witnesses entrust to reliable men who will also be qualified to teach others **(II Tim. 2:2).**

Just prior to His ascension into heaven. Jesus Christ gave His small band of faithful followers one of the most important commands of His earthly ministry. The effective fulfillment of this command would determine the success of growth of the kingdom of God in this age. The command, often referred to as the Great Commission, is found in **Matthew 28:18-20:**

> Then Jesus came to them and said, *All authority* in *heaven* and on *earth* has been given *to me.* Therefore *go* and *make disciples* of *all* nations, *baptizing* them in the name of the Father and of the Son and of the Holy Spirit, and *teaching them to obey* everything *I* have commanded you. And surely *I will be with you* always *to* the very *end of the* age.

An examination of this command reveals some points essential to our understanding of the *Great Commission.* The *focal point of the command is that the main goal is to make disciples. This seemingly obvious truth has some important implications to any Christian sincerely desiring to fully obey his Lord.*

First, the command to evangelize is nowhere given. Yet evangelism is the usual emphasis derived from this passage. Since the first *step in making a disciple is to win a person to Christ,* it would be a terrible mistake to stop there and never go beyond the communication of the gospel. *We are commanded to make disciples, not merely adherents, as the product of our ministries.* By stating the command the way He did, Christ insured a perspective on ministry that went *beyond the initial step of evangelism.* Since we are a people addicted to short-cuts, such a precaution was necessary.

A second implication of Christ's command is that the means of achieving the Great Commission depends not so much on better techniques and greater technology, but rather on the development of committed people. This multiplication of disciples is commanded because people are reached for Christ most effectively through other people. The reality of the gospel, of new life in Christ, is not so much written about as lived. *The divine plan for saturating our world with the gospel is through the multiplication of people who are committed to the lordship of Christ in all aspects of their lives.*

At first glance it seems strange that the Lord would choose this plan. Human beings are so much less reliable than machines and much more prone to error. It would seem that there are too many variables in them to make it wise to stake something as crucial as the Great Commission on their faithfulness. Yet this is exactly what God has done—with one important addition: *He is with us in this work.* The fulfillment of the Great Commission is not a self-effort project. The authority and power of heaven are at our disposal in the accomplishing of this divine command. *Through the enabling power of the Holy Spirit, the impossible becomes possible.* And it is at this point that the strategy begins to make sense. *The clearest way to see the reality of the gospel message is to see the mature believer demonstrating the* fruits of the Spirit in his life and in his relationships with *non-Christians.* In fact, this was part of the value of the incarnation of Christ—we were able to see the divine in human terms we could comprehend. The assurance of God with us makes all the difference.

First, *to be growing in Christ, a Christian must meet*

certain conditions. He must have a basic understanding of his faith, have a regular devotional time, be involved in good fellowship, and be instructed in the Word of God. Second, the Christian desiring to grow in Christ must be obeying and applying what God has commanded him through the Bible. Such a life style of obedience is basic to true discipleship. Third, they must receive regular training in the practical aspects of outreach and ministry so that they can be fruitful and conserve that fruit.

The goal of our disciple-building work could be summarized in another way by saying we are seeking to produce a transferrer, or a teacher. *A true disciple is a teacher in the sense that one is involved in communicating the truth of God's Word to others on a personal level.* The Great Commission clearly include this idea of teaching and building teachers. It is therefore imperative that we work to produce individuals capable of teaching others if the process of disciple building is to continue beyond ourselves. **Hebrew 5:11,12** is a classic passage which shows that the production of teachers is the legitimate goal of our disciple building, and something is seriously wrong when this is not achieved.

> We have much to say about this, but it is hard to explain because you are slow to learn. In fact, though by this time you ought to be teachers, you need someone to teach you the elementary truths of God's word all over again.

Disciple building was also Paul's goal in his instruction to Timothy **(II Timothy 2:2):**

> And the things what you have heard me say in the presence of many witnesses entrust (teach) to reliable men who will also be qualified to teach others.

Such a ministry is summarized by the concept of multiplication. One disciple must be developing other disciples, who in turn can develop other disciples. It is the concept of multiplication which underlies the purpose of this book. *Multiplying disciples is the only way to effectively fulfill the Great Commission, and disciples are best produced through discipleship training.*

For multiplication to occur, a mature Christian must make a conscious decision to work in discipleship training with new Christians. Multiplication is a process that goes through four distinct phases.

Phase one is simply to evangelize. This phase focuses on our personally sharing of our faith with the non-Christian world around us. When fruit results from your evangelism, you are ready to begin phase two of the multiplication process.

Phase two of the multiplication process is doing personal follow-up with an individual who has repented and believed in Christ as Savior. Once a Christian has been stabilized, you are ready to begin the third phase in the multiplication process.

The disciple being developed must actually be involved in training others, in reproducing what he/she has learned in the lives of others.

Phase four occurs when the person with whom you are working actually succeeds in producing other disciples. This is when 2 Timothy 2:2 becomes a reality in your ministry. True multiplication only occurs when you have reached phase four. At this stage the person with whom you are working proves his/her faithfulness and commitment.

The Great Commission is never really going to be fulfilled until multiplication is achieved.

The following statistical study clearly show the far-reaching effect of such an intensive, multiplying ministry. An evangelism contact figure is also given, based on an average of fifty contacts per year for each multiplying disciple:

Year One
1. Begin year: 1 disciple (you)
2. End year: 2 disciples (you, plus 1)
3. Evangelistic contacts: 50

Year Two
1. Begin year: 2 disciples
2. End year: 4 disciples
3. Evangelistic contacts: 100

Year Three
    1. Begin year: 4 disciples
    2. End year: 8 disciples
    3. Evangelistic contacts: 200

Year Four
    1. Begin Year: 8 disciples
    2. End year: 16 disciples
    3. Evangelistic contacts: 400

Year Five
    1. Begin year: 16 disciples
    2. End year: 32 disciples
    3. Evangelistic contacts: 800

Year Six
    1. Begin year: 32 disciples
    2. End year: 64 disciples
    3. Evangelistic contacts: 1,600

Continued at this rate, multiplication will produce 1,024 disciples and the annual confrontation with the gospel of over 25,000 people after ten years. This fantastic fruitfulness can result directly from your disciple ministry, even though you will only have worked with ten people over the decade. *The only real variable is whether you work in such a way as to produce truly reproducing disciples.*

Manpower shortages and ineffective gospel penetration in the community can be corrected by disciple building multiplication.

Chapter 5

The Ministry of Discipleship in Modern Society

The Church — Social Club or Ministry

Juan Carlos Ortiz, in the marvelous book *Discipleship* tells of a rude awakening he had concerning what and where the church ought to be. Despite unusual success in ministry, Ortiz had grown tentative about his direction, uneasy despite the church's increased numbers and activities and frustrated with developing new programs each year only to have to redesign them the next year. With the concurrence of this church he took off time to devote to prayer and meditation and to seek clear direction from the Lord. He took time off to try to recover a plausible or enabling piety.

It was during this time that Ortiz discovered, as persons of dedication, faith and vision have always discovered, that while we seek the Lord, He is already searching for us. And He will find us where we are. He found Moses on the backside of a mountain tending sheep. He found Amos as He dressed sycamore trees and tended His farm. He found Isaiah in the temple in His hour of despair , and if he choose to encounter us, he will find us where we are. Thus Juan Carlos heard the Lord Speak:

> Juan, where is my finger in all this? You are
> dealing with my things —
> And you are promoting them as Coca-Cola
> Promotes its products, as reader's digest
> sells records and books. The letters, the finger?

After reflection, he discovered that he could not discern the spirit of the Lord anywhere in his ministry, only the things he had learned in seminars, conferences, conventions, books and workshop or at the feet of other preachers. Despite the fact that he could point with pride to the obvious success of His tactics — a church that had grown from 200 to 600 in two years — the Lord said to him:

> **You are not growing, You are just getting fat. You just have more people of the same kind. You had 200 without love ... Now 600 — all Without love ... More of the Same ... Not growing ... Getting fat.**

And the truth is that our churches, for the most part, are not growing, they're just getting fat.The Lord further challenged Ortiz:

> **"Yours is not a church; it is an orphanage. No one there has a parent; All are orphans and you are the director of an orphanage. Sundays, you fill a bottle of milk and say, "Now open you mouth. And you think you are feeding your people."**

This revelation to Ortiz would not be disturbing if it addressed only an isolated incident in an isolated corner of the world; but if we are truthful, most of us could be included in this story with just a change of names and numbers. The truth is that each of us has known the uneasiness that comes from knowing that we **are not getting the maximum** from the **potential place under our stewardship.** Each of us has known the experience of beginning the year with a new program only to discover that , that program has worked no better than the **"NEW"** program we had last year. *Most of us **have become tentative about our direction for ministry** and how to make it more meaningful in these times and relevant for the days ahead.*

And rather than turn to **some modern day artist of ministry,** or **some seer of new age** ministry or **some prophet of promotion** and production, *let us go to Him who majored in church building* and mastered the act of ministry: the one who is ministry — even our Lord and Savior, Jesus the Christ.

There is a word from Him on what we ought to be and what we must be about *if we* are to move from our current status of:

> —spiritual orphanages to become His church
> —warehousing members to sending forth saints
> —a social club to a militant force
> —exclusiveness to inclusiveness
> —Barrenness to fruitfulness
> —fragmentation to wholeness
> —do-nothingness to do-somethingness
> —the guttermost to the uttermost
> —lukewarmness to "fire shut-up in our bones"

If we are to master the art of discipleship for modern times, we are, if you will, to discover a plausible piety.

In Matthew's gospel in the 28th chapter, verses 18-20, Jesus gives us clear and simple directions that offer us an answer for our anxieties. A cure for our confusion and deliverance from a dilemma. He tells us:

> **All power is given unto me in heaven and in earth. Go ye therefore and teach all nations, baptizing then in the name of the Father, and of the Son, and of the Holy Ghost: Teaching them to observe all things whatsoever I have commanded you: And lo, I am with you always, even unto the end of the world.**

And I believe that Jesus's commission delivered on a mountain a long time ago offers us three bits of illumination that will enable us to make disciples for modern times, thereby embracing an enabling piety.

To make disciples for these modern times, Jesus implies that **we must be connected to and empow-**

ered by Him. (John 15:5):

> **He that abideth in me, and I in Him, the same bringeth forth much fruit; For without me ye can do nothing.** John further defines this empowerment as kinship.**(John 1:12):**
> **But as many as received Him, to them gave *His power* to become the sons of God.**

In many of our assemblies, meetings and gatherings, if preconditions are not met and if the atmosphere is not right, His spirit will not be there. He will be there watching your actions, but His *sanctioning presence* will not be there; *He will* be looking on, but *His enlightening presence* will not be there; He will be there knocking on the door of your heart, but *His strengthening* presence, *His directing presence, His protecting presence,* His *consoling presence,* His *revitalizing presence,* His *comforting presence, and His anointing presence* will not be there. If things are not right, He will not be there. His *empowering presence* will not be there. If God does not approve of what is going on, we will not be connected and empowered. God does not get excited about crowds, money or food. These do not attract the presence of God. But when we belong to Him; when we assemble in His name and we have a common agenda that glorifies Christ — only then will we be connected and empowered. When we are not connected and empowered we:

    —preach and don't believe what we preach
    —teach and don't live what we teach
    —recite creeds and don't know what it means to do a good deed
    —talk but we don't communicate
    —exist but we don't live
    —sing and don't feel what we sing
    —mis-prioritize our values
    —warp our thinking
    —subsume our integrity
    —blur our vision

—jeopardize our souls
—materialize our ministry
—secularize our church
—glorify sex
—deify man
—mutilate the Bible
—shoot canon balls on Sunday and throw snow
   balls on Monday

Man Without God Is Like A Seed upon The Wind

We can get so caught up in "Church Work" that we lose connection with Him who is the *foundation,* the *Chief Cornerstone, Architect* and *Builder of the church.* When we are not connected and empowered we end up with

—Tricky Trustees
—Devilish Stewards and Stewardesses
—Rebellious Choir Members
—Unruly Ushers
—Pimping Preachers
—Picky Pew Sitters
—Messy Missionaries,

The truth is, as E. Stanley Jones said, **"You can't influence others to commit their lives unto Jesus, until first you do."**

We, as ministers of the gospel, must strive to be Christlike ourselves. But we have gotten caught up on the world's standard of success, even as ministers. We've adopted a plastic success model of ministry in which,

—A whoop is more important then substance (I didn't   say don't whoop)
—Style is more important than content
—Dress is more impressive than virtue

But I heard Jesus say, **"what shall it profit a man to gain the whole world and lose His soul."** What does it profit a man to have a

$700 suit	but	No character
$200 Hat	but	No integrity
$300 Shoes	but	No self-discipline
$ 75 Shirt	but	No purpose
$ 60 Tie	but	No compassion
$ 50 Shirt	but	No brains

"Man shall not live by bread alone ..."
"Seek ye first the kingdom of God and its righteousness.
"Jesus industry/firm the price is right"
"Days get brighter—burdens get lighter as I journey"
"Foxes have holes and birds have nest but the son of man has not a place to lay his head."

And thinking, living and acting that runs counter to the call of Jesus tends to separate us from Him who is the source of our strength. Our focus and power must be connected and empowered.

Jesus tells us that if we are to make disciples we must ***"Go and make them."*** **The Lord says Go,** to the poor and those burdened in spirit, with blurred down horizons and lost hope. **The Lord says Go,** to the disconnected, disaffected, dispossessed, despairing, disenchanted, discouraged, disinherited, dejected, degraded, disrespected, disadvantaged, despondent, devitalized and depersonalized.

There was another time in the life of the church when the Lord told the church to **go** — only to discover that its so easy for us to become comfortable sitting around Jerusalem— maintaining the Temple. Many times the church can be pictured as men sitting around fishing in an Aquarium ignoring the bounty of the ocean just a short distance away. Thus we end up swapping members and guarding jealously those in our care while thousands march pass our doors everyday on their way to hell. Fishing in an Aquarium — the ocean is out there but we remain comfortable fishing in an Aquarium.

This is why Jesus told Peter and others to launch out into the deep. Get out of the shallow waters.

Part of the dilemma we face is that many people, we should be seeking, don't fit our image of what material the Lord can use to make disciples. As John R. Mott said, **"The greatest hindrance to the evangelization of the world are those within the church."**

But we must come to accept, not just in our mind, but in our heart.

As Henry Ward Beecher points out, "The Church is not a Gallery for the exhibition of eminent (saints), But a school for the education of imperfect ones."

If we had been in charge of Jesus' personnel committee, none of the original disciples would have been included in the ministry.

> —A liar named **Peter**
> —A betrayer named **Judas**
> —A doubting **Thomas**
> —A prejudice **Nathaniel**
> —The ill-tempered **James and John**
> —A thief named **Matthew**

Jesus chose from among the *left outs, drop outs* and *put outs* of society: "The whole have no need of a Physician, I have not come to call the righteous but sinners to repentance" (Luke 5:31,32).

People with problems need the church just like sick people need a hospital.

And if the truth is told and we look at who and what He still uses, none of us are just right. **Former *liars* and *hypocrites*, *pool hustlers* and *bar flies*, *back sliders* and *ramblers*, *gossipers*, gigolos, pimps and backbiters, living our lives in air-conditioned Hell and wall-to-wall misery.** Sometimes we have to be reminded "All have sinned and fallen short of the glory of God." Charles Morison was right when He said that:

> **The Christian Church is the only society in the world in which membership is based upon the qualification that the candidate shall be *unworthy* of membership.**

And we must be reminded that by Grace "Are ye saved through faith and not of yourselves, it is the gift of God." The Lord has entrusted to us the responsibility to go:

> —Go tell the story that's old but forever new
> —Tell a dying world that "the wages of sin is death, but the gift of God is Eternal life."
> —Tell somebody that "God so loved the world that He gave His only begotten son."
> —Tell somebody that "they that wait upon the Lord shall renew their strength."
> —Tell somebody that "All things work together for good to them that love the Lord."
> —Tell the world that death has been defeated and the grave has been overcome.

And when they hear and come crying "What must I do to be saved," We are to teach, instruct — but more accurately — *We are to disciple them into the community of faith.*

Too often we are content to make church members and not disciples because it is easier and its all that some of us know. *"Give your heart to Jesus and your hand to the preacher."*

Jesus never made it easy for people to join His movement:

> If any man would come after me let Him deny himself, take up his cross and follow me (Matthew 16:24). Go and make disciples.
> Go and sell all that you have, give it to the poor and come and follow me (Matthew 19:21).
> Let the dead bury their dead, and come and follow me (Matthew 8:22).
> Except a man eat my flesh and drink my blood He can have no part of me (John 6:53).

There is no "CHEAP GRACE" as Bonhoeffer would say. Jesus knew that there are significant differences between members and disciples.

Think about it — it doesn't take much commitment, sacrifice or effort to be a member. The requirements are to:

> —Pay dues
> —Attend church — sometimes
> —Keep basic rules of conduct of the club

But discipleship requires much more of those who would be and those who would disciple them.

It requires interrelatedness and interdependence.

> "Let the strong bear the infirmities of the weak." "Brethren if a man be overcome in a fault ye which are spiritual restore such as one."

Too often our churches are like social clubs and maintenance operations. So much of our time is spent in "Church work and so little in ministry. In the average church 90% of time is spent in fund-raising activities and maintenance of the church program and only ten percent in ministry.

But ministry should be our prime objective and producing persons those equipped to minister its corollary. William Adams Brook is right when he said, "The church exists to train its member through the practice of the presence of God to be servants of others, to the end that Christlikeness may become common property."

As he began his ministry Jesus stood in the Synagogue and read:

> The spirit of the Lord is upon me because he has anointed me to preach the gospel to the poor, *He hath* sent me to heal the broken hearted, to preach deliverance to the captives and *recovery* to sight to the blind, *to set* at liberty them that are bruised. . .

And we have perverted His intent by our actions to say:

To preach the gospel to those who come to
  church
To fix the broken furnace
To raise funds through chicken dinners
To pay off the mortgage through tricks and gim-
  micks
To put down those who do not agree with us.

We are to teach the unsearchable riches of the kingdom and challenge those we lead to put faith into
action; To demonstrate love by how we live; To be peace
makers in a troubled world; the salt of the earth; a city
set upon a hill and light shining in darkness. We are to
go and make disciples. We must challenge:

—The sleepy to wake up
—The crooked to straighten up
—The meek to speak up
—The stingy to give it up
—The despairing to look up
—The liar to fess up

All to the glory and honor of God who lives in us, we
are to go to the hedges and highways:

The brood streets and back alleys
The suburbs and public housing
Sugar hill and sorrow's valley

Teaching, preaching and reaching everybody we can
for the cause of Jesus Christ.

Conclusion

When we are empowered by Christ and then go and make disciples, the Lord's promise is that He will be with us. He is the same yesterday, today and forever.

—Parents change,	but Jesus is the same
—Weather changes,	but Jesus is the same
—Friends change,	but Jesus is the same
—Room-mates change,	but Jesus is the same
—School-mates change,	but Jesus is the same
—Cars change,	but Jesus is the same
—Grades change,	but Jesus is the same
—Taste buds change,	but Jesus is the same
—Bodies change,	but Jesus is the same
—Churches change,	but Jesus is the same
—Pastors change,	but Jesus is the same
—Bishops change,	but Jesus is the same
—Laypersons change,	but Jesus is the same

He is the same yesterday, today and forever. This statement **destroys TRANSUBSTANTIATION.** *This doctrine teaches that every time the mass is stated by the Priest, the bread and wine become the body and blood of Jesus. This is not necessary. The same Jesus that died for us once and for all on Calvary does not need to die every time we come to the communion table. He had to die only one time for our sins.*

This truth demolishes a unitarian Christology which says that each one of us can become a little Christ. No, there is only one Lord, one faith and one baptism. Jesus is the same yesterday, today and forever. There is nobody like my Jesus. There is nobody like my Lord. He will be with you.

This truth defeats the teaching of process theology which talks about a growing God who is growing and maturing with His creation. Our Christ is not the creation. Our Christ does not grow with nor is limited by His creation. *He is* timeless one, and in Him all things are held together. *He is* the originator and the consummation of human history. This axiom disposes of the philosophy of **Deism** which says that *the stage of history is Godless,* but you and I know Christ is Emmanuel. He is with me; He walks with me —talks with me.

Bishop Stephen Neill has written a theology of the New Testament entitled *Jesus Through Many Eyes.* He says that after the middle of the first century there are *five great centers of Christological preaching.* Each center emphasized a distinctive truth, but they all were preaching about the same Jesus. These centers were *Jerusalem, Antioch, Ephesus, Alexandria, and Rome.* No one center of preaching and no single theological emphasis could fully capture all that Jesus is.

Jesus is more than any pen can write or any tongue can tell, Orators, whose sentences are flight of golden arrows, express only a meager measure of the honor due him. **Writers,** words falling from their pens like golden pollen from stems of shaken lilies, feel the inadequacy of all words to set Him forth in His beauty. **Profound scholars,** researching with angelic passion through mysterious realms of theology, fail in their quest to tell us all about Jesus. **Musicians** who create majestic hymns, matchless anthems, moving spirituals, and modern gospel songs feel inadequate in describing the Lamb of God who is also the lion of the tribe of Judah. That is why musicians will sing a new song in the new Jerusalem. **No Architect** can ever design a Cathedral that will give full honor to Jesus. All that can be said or done was given to us by the writer of this truth, "Jesus is the same yesterday, today, and forever."

This is why we call Jesus, **Master.** Only the master can say:

> Come unto me, All ye that labour and are heavy laden, and I will give you rest. Take my yoke upon you, and learn of me ... For my yoke is easy, and my burden is light **(Matt. 11:28,30)**

The Master speaks three important verbs to us. They are all in the imperative mood. **"Come, learn ,go."**

Because Jesus is still the same yesterday, today and tomorrow, we can **still come to Him.** We can **still learn of Him.** We can **still go and serve Him.**

He is the Master. **When He speaks, nature obeys.** The **lightning ceases** to play its glimmer game on the bosom of the clouds. **When He speaks** the thunder ceases to play the volcanic roar of bass drums in nature's symphony orchestra. And **singing winds give up their melodic sounds** that make mighty trees bend to their harmonic breezes. **When He speaks** the salty sea slaps rock-ribbed coast lines with misty sprays that fall to soak the sand and all nature behaves itself at the sound of His voice, so that the raging sea is transformed into a mirror of glass that reveals the silver reflections of the moon which presides as the queen of night. **When He speaks** demons vacate human lives, **Sauls become** Pauls, and **Jezebels** becomes Esthers. **When He spoke** in creation, **The morning** stars sang together, and the sons of God shouted for joy. When He spoke in the manger at Bethlehem, sleeping prophecy woke up to see the light shining in the darkness. **When He spoke at Calvary** justice cried **out, "The old account is settled." When He spoke at Pentecost** the prophet Joel said, "at last my prophecy is fulfilled."

When that same Jesus speaks in the Eschatological future **Isaiah will say to Joel:** "Now my prophecy is fulfilled: **"The wolf** will live with the lamb, **The leopard** will lie down with the goat, **The calf and the loin and the yearling** together, and **a little child** will lead them. The **infant** will play near the hole of the cobra, and the **young child** shall put his hand into the viper's nest. "They will neither harm nor destroy on all my Holy mountain, for the earth will be full of the knowledge of the Lord as the waters cover the sea" **(Isa. 11:69, NIV).**

> —He will be with you in school
> —When money is low
> —Car is out of fix
> —In the sunshine and the rain
> —In bright days and dark nights
> —In times of joy and times of trial

—In sickness and in health
—Up the rough side of the mountains
—And down into the valley

This same Jesus who is the *Lily of the valley.* This ageless Christ, in an aging world, the same yesterday, today and tomorrow. He will be with you:

—Who is king of kings
—Who is Alpha and Omega
—Who is Captain of the Lord's Host
—Who is a rock in a weary land
—Who is bridge over troubled water

This same Jesus:

Who was born in a lowly manger
Who grew up in little Nazareth
Who walked the dusty roads of Palestine
Who taught like a teacher
Healed like a doctor

This same Jesus

*Who was arrested in Gethsemane's garden
Who was led from judgment hall to judgment
Who bore the cross up Calvary
Whom they stretched wide and hung high
Who died for you and me Jesus

And early on a Sunday morning

Got up and proclaimed:
"All power is given unto me" — Connected now —all power — empowered now — I am pious now

This same Jesus:

At whose name every knee shall bow and tongue confess Who sits at the right hand of the Father

Will be with us:

Till the sun refuses to shine
The moon drips away in blood
Shiloh comes and peace is ours
Death is overcome and the grave made empty
The end of the age.

Chapter 6
Understanding the Eqipping Ministry

The Basic Premise

What is the equipping ministry? How does it differ from more traditional concepts of ministry? How does a pastor change his style of leadership? What may be learned from New Testament models of ministry? Why is the equipping ministry so important?

The purpose of this section is to answer these and other significant questions related to the ministry of Christ's church. Actions are directly motivated by our concepts. If our understanding is accurate, then our behavior can be altered to reflect our comprehension.

Many congregations have never examined their thinking regarding the role of a pastor in light of New Testament teaching. Through tradition and practice, they have formed a general idea about the way a "good" minister functions. If the present pastor conforms to their ideas about the ministry, then he/she is welcome to remain with the congregation. On the other hand, if his style of ministry is not acceptable, he must change his ways or move to a new field of service.

Such practice never deals with the root of the problem. Suppose both the minister and the congregation have a faulty attitude about the way he/she should function. Then what? Who is to blame? If alterations are needed, who will initiate them? Furthermore, how can they decide whose views are correct?

Our basic concept of leadership in the church must come from the Scripture. Most congregations today employ a paid leader to minister for them, where as in the New Testament, the primary purpose of a leadership ministry is to equip the congregation to minister **(Ephesians 4:12).**

This section calls for a very important turnaround in the thinking of the average church. Some in the congregation will respond with a "ho hum" or "so what". On the other hand, those who really care about the mission of Christ through the church will see this fundamental shift in thinking as extremely vital. It is one of the basic keys to church growth and world evangelization. It is also a critical step toward congregational harmony and outreach.

The Equipping Ministry Of Jesus

The essential concept of ministry in the church stems from the life and work of Jesus himself. "The Son of man," He said," came not to be served but to serve (Mark 10:45). This summary statement is very important in any study of the equipping ministry.

Although the accounts in the four Gospels are tantalizingly brief, we know that Jesus practiced an equipping kind of leadership on earth. How did He go about it? First of all, He found others to minister. "He found Phillip," John records, "and said to him, 'Follow me'" (:43). Jesus continued to discover others who could minister. Some turned away because they would not meet the stringent demands of work in the kingdom (Luke 9:57-62).

Jesus equipped others to minister by loving them **(John 13:34)**, by teaching them **(Matthew 5:2)**, by praying for them **(Luke 22:39-41)**, and by training them on the job **(Matthew 10:5ff, Luke 10:1ff)**.

The preparation of ministers was a major concern of Jesus. Why? Could He not be satisfied with spectacular results of His own work? Thousands followed Him from place to place. He could scarcely find time to sleep or eat. Sometimes it was necessary for Him to flee from the multitudes. His name became a household word. Why then did He call others to service?

Consider the purpose of the relationship of Jesus with His disciples. Of course, they enjoyed His masterful teaching. Of course, there were lazy days on the Sea of Galilee with great fellowship and laughter. Of course, He loved them and they loved Him. They were His friends **(John 15:15)**. But the purpose of it all — what was the purpose of it all?

The mission of the twelve and of the seventy gives us a clue. Matthew says, "These twelve Jesus sent out" **Matthew (10:5)**. Luke writes, "After this the Lord appointed seventy others, and sent them on ahead of him" **Luke** (10:1). *They were called to be sent.* Here we have a significant key to the ministry of Jesus. He equipped others to perform a ministry of their own.

The Equipping of Paul

The apostle Paul also practiced an equipping ministry. Some are prone to think of the great missionary to the Gentiles as a "lone eagle," traveling in solitude throughout the Mediterranean basin with his message of salvation. What are the facts?

Actually, Paul carried on a kind of "walking seminary" throughout his missionary journeys. He surrounded himself with those who could later go out on their own. At Lystra, he found Timothy to accompany him **(Acts 16:3)**. Luke recorded that others had been enlisted in the Pauline band: "Sopater of Beroea, the son of Phyrrhus, accompanied him; and of the Thessalonians, Aristarchus and Secundus; and Gaius of Derbe, and Timothy; and the Asians, Tcyhicus and Trophimus" **(Acts 20:4)**.

Here was a small congregation Paul took with him as he traveled. Later Crescens and Demas joined the group, along with others. Mark, who started with him on the first journey and went home, later returned to the work. After mentioning Demas who deserted the cause, Paul wrote, "Crescens has gone to Galatia, Tutus to Dalmatia. Luke alone is with me. Get Mark and bring him with you; for he is very useful in serving me. Tychicus I have sent to Ephesus" **(II Tim. 4:10-12)**.

These Scriptures indicate the kind of equipping ministry which Paul practiced. He found potential leaders as he traveled from city to city. In many cases, they were invited to accompany him, and they learned as they traveled. Later on, they were directed to their own place of ministry. Paul was true to the "equipping concept" which he sets forth in **Ephesians 4:11**.

In his writing, Paul kept in mind those whom he was equipping for ministry. He insisted that Timothy pay strict attention to Scripture since it is "profitable for teaching, for reproof, for correction, and for training in righteousness, that the man of God may be complete, equipped for every good work" **(II Tim. 3:16)**.

The church will always be in debt to Barnabas who

helped sponsor Paul in his early ministry. Shunned by the disciples because they knew his reputation for persecuting Christian, Paul found in Barnabas the mentor he needed in his rise to leadership. This incident points up a real test of the equipping ministry. What happens when we recruit those whose abilities eclipse our own? Do we encourage them, or seek to thwart them in their mission?

Are We Prepared For Change?

In order for our local churches to begin operating on the principles of the equipping ministry, some changes will be necessary.

A historian remarked about Woodrow Wilson that he "made no fetish of the god of things as they are." Those who are satisfied with the concept of ministry now held by the majority of Christian Methodists will not be interested in changing. On the other hand, Christians who are feeling frustrated and defeated by our present system of ministry will welcome a more scriptural approach.

Every preaching minister needs to know where he/she stands in his/her own thinking regarding the equipping concept. He/She must realize the different nature of this procedure. He/She cannot lead the local church on a pilgrimage when he/she is unsure of his/her own direction. Hazy thinking on his/her part is certain to be sensed and reflected throughout the church.

Sometimes a preaching minister feels a non-equipping ministry will work in the congregation if he/she tries harder and puts in more hours. When the basic concept itself is faulty, however, then change must be made on a deeper level.

Fundamental to our thinking must be the New Testament precept and precedent— every Christian is a minister of Jesus Christ. Peter refers to his readers as a "royal priesthood" and calls them to the responsibility of declaring "the wonderful deeds of him who called you out of the darkness into his marvelous light" **(I Peter 2:9).** In the book of Revelation, John spoke about the ascended Christ who has "made us a kingdom, priest to his God and Father" **Revelation (1:6).** The idea of every Christian being a minister for Christ is finally dawning upon the American Church.

However, faced with the advent of an equipping ministry, some preaching ministers experience an identity crisis. If everyone is a minister," they reason, "then what is important for me to do?" They ask, "What distinctive role do I have with a congregation?" Such questions are understandable. The work of the preaching minister takes on new lustre, however, when he/she is fulfilling his/her rightful vocation. He/She is the one who has usually received special training for his/her work. He/She is a "professional" in the best sense of the word. There will always be the need for a paid career minister in the church.

The minister's work is to set about helping others in the congregation to minister. He/She must know something about the spiritual qualifications and the capabilities of each person he/she "equips." When he/she knows the people, and loves them for their own worth, he/she can begin preparing them for their ministry.

The equipping ministry, properly conducted, will incorporate both Biblical and sociological principles of leadership. It is not a leadership-leveling process. Every person has a different degree of leadership. A shared leadership within the church is certainly a Biblical concept, but the idea of "equal influence" is not. Some have more influence than others. Paul had more influence than Barnabas. Peter, James, and John evidently had the most leadership ability among the twelve. The writer of Hebrews is not contradicting the concept of the equipping ministry when he admonishes his readers to "remember you leaders, those who spoke to you the word of God" **(Hebrew 13:7).**

It is taken for granted that preaching ministers will have a marked influence on the life of a church. The important thing is how they use such influence. Some ministers walk softly at first, then later carry a "big stick." Once they have control, woe to the person who opposes them on any detail! Their will reigns supreme.

In a time of war, Congress grants the President of the United States almost dictatorial powers. When the crisis is over, however, the same Congress redistributes these powers. The nation's founding fathers saw the dangers of a government without checks and balances.

This principle is applicable to the church. Paul evidently entrusted Titus with some very strong powers in

Crete **(Titus 1:5).** It is foolish to assume, though, that Paul is here repealing the New Testament procedure of selecting Church leadership with the aid of the congregation **(Acts 6:3).**

The preaching minister who is accustomed to making all decisions must gradually begin to relinquish some authority to others. A "ruling elder" may need to do the same. Members of the congregation who have been mere passive sheep must become active with the shepherds in "building up the body of Christ" **(Ephesians 4:12).**

Early attempts to perform an equipping ministry for a congregation may be checked by "starts" and "stops". Such dramatic change will not happen overnight. Churches must have time to adjust to the new style of leadership. The equipping ministry, however, when accepted and implemented by the church, will unleash new impetus for the gospel which most of us have only dreamed about. It can change the world by putting flesh on the dry bones in the valley, of which rumor has it that they are dead. Nothing drives the rumor out of the church like a good sound Biblical equipping ministry.

Chapter 7
Equipping and Developing Leadership

David Lowes Watson in his book **Forming Christian Disciples** reminds us that the leadership of the United Methodist Church held an international gathering at Fort Worth, Texas in 1990. The leadership called the church to a new vision entitled: **Vital Congregation—Faithful Disciples.** They declared that the people of God called Methodists have traveled the religious journey to a critical turning in their rich history. They were challenge by their leadership to follow Jesus Christ into a new era:

> The church is the people called to witness to God's saving action in Jesus Christ. God offers to all who will believe an infinite, redeeming love made known in the cross and in the resurrection of Jesus Christ. As the resurrection promises, God intends to transform this world into a new creation. When that time comes, God will be all in all, and people will live together in wholeness, harmony, justice, and peace. The church is the community of those who expect that new creation and whose actions point toward its coming. 'The kingdom of God has come near," Jesus announced **(Mark 1:15)** and so the church proclaims today through every word and deed.

The leadership further declared that the only way for Christians to serve as heralds of this kingdom is to place Christ at the center of the church's life and work. Only as Christ's ministry is active through congregational mission and personal discipleship can the church see the new direction in which God is leading. Those of us called Methodists will be vital congregations and faithful disciples only as we join with one another around the world but in proclaiming our hope in Jesus Christ's ministry and mission today.

Concomitant with the gathering of the United Methodists in 1990 at Fort Worth, Texas was the Christian Methodists meeting in 1990 at Arlington, Texas where during the session of the General Conference our leadership called upon the total membership in the address to become true disciples of Jesus Christ. The College of Bishops and the General Officers of our church carried this vision further when they called upon each member of our beloved Zion to help implement the Discipleship 2000 plan.

This plan calls for our church to make discipleship the "center piece" of all our Christian Education training sessions on all levels.

The CME Church must make disciples of its members. **(Matthew 28:19-20).** Prior to His ascension into heaven, Jesus Christ gave His small circle of disciples one of the most important and profound commands of His earthly ministry. The effective fulfillment of this command would determine the success of growth of the Kingdom of God. This commandment is often referred to as the Great Commission. The focal point of the command is that the main goal is to make disciples. Gary W. Kuhne, in his book, *THE DYNAMICS OF DISCIPLING — BEING AND PRODUCING SPIRITUAL LEADERS*, gives us a meaningful and accurate definition of a disciple; "A disciple is a Christian who is growing in conformity to Christ, is achieving fruit in evangelism and is walking in follow-up to conserve His fruit".

This is the type of person the CME Church is commanded to develop. A discipled member is one who has a basic understanding of his faith; who has regular devotional time; who is involved in good fellowship; and who is instructed in the Word of God. A discipled member is also one who obeys and applies what God has commanded through the Bible.

We must learn how to make disciples of the laity

effectively. The next decade and the years to come will belong to lay Christians and to the preachers who know how to teach them. The day of clericalism is gradually fading away. Clericalism is the notion that the preacher does all the religious work. Pastors must multiply themselves by training others. We must invest in others as did our mentors. They must become preacher/trainers and we, as Bishops, must continue to be pastor/layperson trainers. The text for the next decade should be **II Tim. 2:1-2:** "As for you my son, be strong through the Grace that is ours in union with Christ Jesus. Take the teachings that you heard me proclaim in the presence of many witnesses and entrust them to reliable people who will be able to teach others".

To give shape to this vision, we charged our church not only to proclaim Jesus as the Christ, but also to exemplify the love and justice of God embodied in Jesus of Nazareth. Vital local church congregations must equip the people of God not only to witness to Christ in everyday living but also to practice care and hospitality. Vital congregations must not only be faithful in the ministries of the word and sacrament instructing people in the Scriptures and fostering the discipline of prayer and fasting, but also in joining with Christ in the ministries of justice, hope and peace. We must obey his commandments to feed the hungry, clothe the naked, visit the sick as well as those in prison and reach out to those who are in pain as well as those who are neglected and sinned against.

If the ministry of Discipleship 2000 is going to be realized, we must began retraining or training our present members and raising up a whole new generation of leaders in our local churches.

Local churches are the basic communities of faith within which new leaders for the church must be identified, called, prepared and supported. The raising up of committed, dedicated imaginative leaders is, in my opinion, a gift of the Holy Spirit and a sign of life in Christ. It is Christ who calls leaders for God's mission in the world and the Holy Spirit who gives them the gifts of leadership. Yes! There are bones in the valley and rumor has it that they are dead. The Spirit of God must blow breath into these bones so that they can get up, connect themselves to their prayer joint and live again. Bones live again when Christ becomes the center of a local church.

"If Christ is not the center of everything the church is trying to do and attempts to be, then its light is hidden under a bushel, its salt lacks taste, its leaven is inert and its seed is barren." Christ and Christ alone must be honored by disciples who wish to be faithful, and He must be at the center of congregations that wish to be vital. The only way for this to be accomplished is for local leaders to accept responsibility for becoming Christian disciples and for the local church as a whole to acknowledge and respect their leadership.

Re-traditioning Classes and Class Leaders

The source of the new leadership for which the CME Church is calling is found in the Methodist traditions of class meetings and class leaders, both of which have been long neglected and much misunderstood. The time has come to "tradition" them again; to go back to their origins, to see them in *their historical context,* to re-interpret them in light of the gospel, and to re-appropriate them for the ministry and mission of Jesus Christ in the world of today.

The Context For Leadership

We must learn how to *introduce and develop covenant discipleship groups as the context for this leadership.* In order to do this we must adhere to the *general rule of Discipleship:* "*To witness to Jesus Christ in the world, and to follow his teachings through acts of compassion, justice, worship, and devotion, under the guidance of the Holy Spirit.*"

These groups provide a context for developing leaders in Discipleship, not because the members excel in their Christian living, nor because they have a closer relationship with Christ. They serve their local churches as role models in discipleship quite simply because *they hold themselves accountable.* They monitor their obedience to Jesus Christ in the company of trusted friends. They understand only too well how easy it is to slip into disobedience—or worse, to form their discipleship around their own preferences rather than the teachings of Jesus.

Implementing Leadership

The way to implement this leadership is by recovering an office that once was the very fiber of Methodism, *the class leader.* Class leaders are those persons in a local church who are willing to help with forming the discipleship of a number of other church members. In turn, class leaders are formed by covenant discipleship. This does not mean that everyone who belongs to a covenant discipleship group should be a class leader; but everyone who is a class leader should belong to a covenant discipleship group.

Recovering this tradition will require some major adjustments, not only on the part of congregations, but also on the part of pastors. Just as they share leadership with laypersons in the administrative and programmatic dimensions of the church's ministry, so pastors will have to accept shared leadership in the forming of Christian disciples. The work of James D. Anderson and Ezra Earl Jones proves timely and helpful in this regard. Distinguishing between *transactional leadership* as that which governs the institutional maintenance of the church. and *transformational leadership* as that which calls and enables the church to live out God's vision for the world, they show how both modes of leadership are necessary for vital congregations and faithful disciples. They also argue convincingly that transactional leadership has come to hold a virtual monopoly in today's congregations, robbing them of God's vision and reducing them to administrative and programmatic institutions.

The recovery of the office of class leader can be an important step toward revitalizing transformational leadership, and thus restoring the necessary balance. But pastors and lay people alike must be ready to accept the hard work this will involve for there can be no shortcuts. The call to faithful discipleship will require the fulfillment of long overdue worldly obligations, rather than yet another quest for supposedly unclaimed spiritual benefits. The call to dry bones to live again will require the acceptance of down-to-earth supervision by hitherto unrecognized lay leadership, rather than yet another round of pastoral rhetoric as a way of avoiding obedience to Jesus Christ in the world. And both of these requirements are likely to occasion a marked degree of initial inconvenience.

If we manage to recover this tradition, however the CME Church may well do more than help ourselves toward faithful discipleship and congregational vitality. We may find that in this distinctive model of lay leadership we have a unique contribution to make to the church at a critical moment in God's saving history.

Early Methodist Role Model

The early Methodist revival was a period that was filled with excellent role models. In the words of the founding leader, John Wesley, the movement had its origins toward the end of 1739, when eight of ten persons came to me in London ... deeply convinced of sin, and earnestly groaning for redemption. They desired (as did two or three more the next day) that I would spend some time with them in prayer, and advise them how to flee from the wrath to come ... . I appointed a day when they might all come together, which from thence forward they did every week, namely, on Thursday, in the evening ... . This was the rise of the United Society, first in London, and "having the form, and seeking the power of godliness, united in order to pray together, to receive the word of exhortation, and to watch over one another in love, that they may help each other to work out their salvation.

As their name implies, the early Methodists were noted for the method of their discipleship. The passage we have just cited come from their **General Rules of 1743,** in which John Wesley laid out some guideline for Christian living in the world, at once very straightforward and practicable. The method consisted of identifying the essential components of Christian discipleship and then making sure they were carried out.

Components of Christian Discipleship

Wesley grouped the components of Christian discipleship under two broad heading: *"works of mercy"* (doing everything possible to *serve God and one's neighbor*, while avoiding those things that offend God and harm one's neighbor); and "works of piety" (doing everything needful to *be pen to God's grace*).

Weekly Accountability

In order to make sure that these works of mercy and piety were actually performed — and, just as important, that they were held in proper balance —the **General Rules** also stipulated *a weekly meeting* for all the society members, at which they were to hold themselves *mutually accountable for their Christian living in the world.* These *weekly gatherings were known as "class meetings."* Wesley described them as the "sinews" of the movement, and there is little doubt that they were the key to the disciplined living of the members.

This straightforward method of discipleship— *the disciplines of seeking God and serving neighbor, held in balance through mutual accountability — is no less practicable today.* Using the early class *meeting as a model, they have formed covenant discipleship groups, which meet for one hour each week so that the members may hold themselves mutually accountable for their discipleship. They do this by writing a covenant, in which they agree on the basics of their Christian living in the world. Then, at their weekly meetings, they go through the covenant, clause by clause, telling each other how they have fared on their Christian pilgrimage since last they were together.*

The General Rules of Discipleship

Some CME Churches have not copied the early class meeting. Rather, *they have "traditioned" it* — that is *they have taken the essence of the class meeting as it functioned in early Methodism, and appropriated it for today in light of the gospel.* In so doing, they have also traditioned the General Rules. taking the essentials of the rules — "works of mercy" and "works of piety" — and appropriated them for the church of today, covenant of discipleship groups have formulated a General Rule of Discipleship:

> To witness to Jesus Christ in the world, and to follow His teachings through acts of compassion, justice, worship, and devotion under the guidance of the Holy Spirit.

TO WITNESS TO JESUS CHRIST means not only proclaiming him as prophet and redeemer, but also calling on all people to acknowledge him as sovereign of the coming reign of God. It means not only obeying the teachings of Jesus, but also making clear whose teachings they are. Jesus left his disciples in no doubt at all that he expected this this testimony from them **(Luke 9:23f)**.

ACTS OF COMPASSION are those simple, basic things we do out of kindness to our neighbor, and our neighbor is anyone who is in need anywhere in the world. To the extent that we feed the hungry, clothe the naked, and visit the sick and the imprisoned, we minister to Christ in our midst.

ACTS OF JUSTICE remind us that God thundered the law from Sinai and pronounced righteousness through the prophets. We must not only minister to people in need, but ask why they are in need in the first place. If they are being treated unjustly, then we must confront the persons or systems that cause the injustice.

ACTS OF WORSHIP are the means of grace that we exercise corporately: the ministries of *word* and *sacra-*

ment. Not only do they *affirm the indispensable place of the church in Christian discipleship,* they also *enable us to build each other up in the Body of Christ.*

ACTS OF DEVOTION are those *private spiritual disciplines of prayer, reading the Scriptures,* and *inward examination,* that bring us face to face with God most directly when no one is present. At such times, our dialogue with God is intensely personal, searching and enriching.

The CME Class Leader: A New Perspective

We honestly and sincerely believe that if our local churches were to return to the class leader system with the right focus it would enhance our ministry of discipleship greatly. The class leader system in the CME Church is one of the best I have seen anywhere. The *Book of Discipline* of the Christian Methodist Episcopal Church, paragraphs 501, 502 and 503, page 139 states as follows:

501. Class leaders shall be appointed by the Preacher in charge. A member from each Class shall be chosen by the Preacher to serve as Class Leader.

502. The moral and spiritual life of the Class Leader shall be as follows:

1. Each of them shall be a person of sound judgment and truly devoted to God.
2. To meet the Ministers and the Stewards of the society once a week in order:
   (a.) To inform the Minister of any that are sick or of any that walk disorderly and will not be reproved.
   (b.) To report to the Stewards what they have received from the members of their several classes, provided, the Leaders collect class dues from each members.

One can readily see that the above description of the class leader's function in the CME Church is congruent with the founding father's original concept, provided that the pastor is enabled and equipped enough to implement it.

So many of our pastors are not prepared to be enabling and equipping disciples; they have no concept of ministry and almost always will not make any special effort to come to the institutes, work-shops and training schools that are provided by Episcopal Districts and the General Church, where they can receive such preparation.

In order for pastors to adequately proclaim the Word and train lay persons today, they must be or become enabling and equipping disciples themselves. Pastors can no longer stand or sit and say, "Lord fill my mouth with fire and stuff and pinch me when I have said enough." The pastor must be a trained disciple; he/she must be adequately prepared to develop class leaders into multiplying disciples. The pastor must, in the words of the late Dr. Blair T. Hunt:

1. Read himself warm
2. Pray himself hot
3. Think himself clear, and
4. Let himself go.

The CME Church has allowed other communions to steal its Holy Ghost thunder its spiritual, systemic dimension, that is to say, its distinctive emphasis on holiness and its class leader system, which, in my humble opinion, is the best discipleship training and development vehicle in the world. Some other denominations have taken our rich, historical concept, changed its name to cell groups, covenant groups, spiritual groups, etc. and are sweeping the country using our original method. That is why we are pleading with you, pastors, "O return ye, o return ye to the class leader system!"

Now, one reason that many people in the CME Church have been turned off by our class leader system is because pastors have used them for everything else except that for which they were intended. Some pastors use them for rallies—Men's Day, Women Day, church anniversaries and pew rallies. Some pastors may even use them for some unwholesome pursuits. The class leader's first obligation is to be a disciple of our Lord and Savior Jesus Christ, then all other things will fall in place. For Jesus has adequately admonished us to "—seek first the kingdom of God and His righteousness, and all these things shall be added to you." **(Matthew 6:33, NKJV).**

The last two phases of our discussion in this chapter on Equipping and Developing Leadership have to do with the class leaders' relationship with other church officers and the important role for class leaders—recognition. In my opinion no one says it better than David Watson:

> Once they are introduced, a crucial aspect of the credibility of class leaders will be to clarify their relationship to other church leaders. Their direct link with the pastor, to say nothing of their appointment by charge conference, is sure to raise questions about the extent to which their responsibilities might duplicate or even conflict with those of other church officers.
>
> The most important clarification is that class leaders provide a complementary role in the congregation. It is helpful in this regard to return to the distinction between transactional and transformational leadership which we discussed earlier. Transformational leadership is responsible for meeting the needs of church members, and for the institutional maintenance of the church. Transactional leadership is responsible for keeping church members focused on the vision of the gospel and the obligations of their discipleship. This is not to say that these two leadership roles are mutually exclusive. Even the most fastidious chairperson of trustees can find a prophetic voice, and even the most visionary pastor

has to deal with air conditioning. But it is to say that the two modes of leadership must be given distinct and equal emphasis in the life and work of the church.

The transactional mode of leadership predominates to the neglect of the transactional. Yet the answer to this in balance does not lie in trying to make administrative and programmatic leaders more transformational. Their mode of leadership must be transactional, because they are responsible for running the church and meeting members' needs. Their energies are already expended in doing precisely that.

Class leaders, by contrast, have the freedom to function in a transformational mode. They are responsible for helping church members grow in their obedience to Jesus Christ. They are also responsible for directing them toward the resources they need in order to live out their discipleship in the world. In this way, they are fully complementary to the transactional leadership of the church.

On the one hand, class leaders need the administrative and programmatic dimensions of the congregation in order to provide resources for their classes. Without these dimensions, the General Rule of Discipleship remains skeletal. On the other hand, their class members must be more intentional in their ministry and mission. If there is any overlap, it is by the way of reinforcing everyone else's work.

In the final analysis, the most important word in the reintroduction of class leaders is "recognition": recognition by the pastor that leaders in discipleship are there in the congregation, waiting to be asked to join in the pastoring of the flock; recognition by the congregation that some of their own members are called to be their leaders in following Christ; and recognition by the class of the highest privileges and responsibilities of the Christian life.

If all of this is recognized, by pastor and people alike, then class leaders will begin to assume their proper place in the congregation; and the preceding guidelines, while helpful perhaps at first, will quickly be left behind. *For the office of class leader is not new.* It was *proven in practice by our Methodist forebearers; it continues in practice among many of our Methodist colleagues;* and it is still *present in the collective memory of a church that badly needs the methodical discipleship it once nurtured.*

The question to be asked, therefore, as a congregation considers incorporating the office of class leader into its life and work, is not whether it *will* work, but whether it *is*. There are countless Methodists, past and present, who have answered that question with a resounding "yes." May there be many others who now decide to join them.

Let the word go forth from this time and place to all Christian Methodists everywhere that the only way will grow numerically and spiritually is for us to implement a strong, serious-minded, Bible-centered and Christ-centered discipleship ministry. We must raise up a new generation of leaders that are receptive to discipleship training. How should we do this? We believe once again that the Methodist tradition holds the answer to our dilemma. A weekly meeting is necessary to develop such leaders in a climate of accountability. Let us return to "the roots of Methodism, a movement first identified by its methodical approach, the precise task of making disciples" — persons who surrender themselves to Jesus Christ; persons who will give a life time of continuing obedience to his teachings in the world under the guidance of the Holy Spirit and a mutual accountability that watches over every member in love.

Structuring the Class System in the Local Church

We have already stated in a broad and general sense the qualifications of the class leader. At this time we will take a more specific look at these qualifications. First, let me remind you that there is no such thing as the "perfect" class leader. In fact, the only perfect small group leader was Jesus Christ, but He was God. We are all imperfect vessels. In spite of this, with the help of the Holy Spirit, one can become a terrific class leader. Some basic qualifications and a clear understanding of the task are essential for success.

Every leadership position within the local church has two fundamental features: (1) the qualifications for service, and (2) the specific task, a job description. Serving as a class leader is no exception. Whereas no one in any church will meet all of the criteria to lead a small group, there are six essential qualifications every small group leader should possess.

(1) An understanding of spiritual — The main point of I Timothy that a new believer should not be given too much responsibility too soon. This is an important principle in selecting class leaders. One must be a Christian for a sufficient length of time. Some people are ready after one year, others may be after five years. The time will vary as it relates to each person, but enough time is needed to understand Christian principles.

(2) A growing relationship with Christ — II Peter 3:18 tells us to "grow in the grace and knowledge of our Lord and Savior Jesus Christ." If the class leader is to model spiritual growth and encourage it in others, it first must be a reality in his life.

(3) A commitment to caring for people — In I Corinthians 12:25 we are instructed to "have the same care for one another." The leader meeting this standard is dedicated to reaching out to the members of the class and helping as needed, comforting them in distressing times, joining them in celebrating their successes, supporting their efforts at self-improvement, and investing time in other activities that express care and concern.

(4) A desire to serve —"Through love serve one another" (Galatians 5:13). A leader is a servant and must be deeply motivated to serve others. Jesus said to His disciples in Matthew 20:27, "And whosoever will be great among you, let him be your servant."

(5) A willingness to learn — "Trying to learn what is pleasing to the Lord" (Ephesians 5:10) applies to everything you do, including service as a class leader. The potential leader may not know everything about being a class leader, but must be willing to learn.

(6) A determination to spend the necessary time — Having the necessary time it takes to be a class leader is an important qualification. Leading the class must "be done properly and in an orderly manner" I Corinthians 14:40). Are you willing to spend the time required to be a class leader?

There are other qualification which could be added to this list, but these are the fundamentals as to what it takes to succeed as a class leader. These six qualifications may be reduced to three by the use of a popular acronym: **F-A-T** people make the best leaders.

F — Faithful to God and your fellow class members
A — Available, having and being willing to spend time
T — Teachable, open to instruction and learning.

Anyone who examines the above list of qualifications for the office of class leader may be somewhat discouraged. Let us remember that God doesn't expect us to be perfect. The potential leader will be strong in certain areas and need further improvement in others. The Holy Spirit will help in the areas of weakness. The Apostle Paul speaks about our ultimate success in Philippians 4:13, "I can do all things through Christ who strengthens me."

Lay Assistant To Pastor

We realize that the class leaders are able to carry out many pastoral functions which may not be considered the best use of the pastor's time. The class leader may even be more effective in many of the day-to-day problems Christians come upon which do not require the specialized training of the pastor. The opportunity is there for the class leader to function in this area. If the church is to fulfill the mandate Jesus left with us, then the office of class leader will lead into discipleship.

They will accept responsibility for other church members more so than any other person in any other leadership position in the church. The leader is a key person in disciplining members as he/she uses his/her gifts and graces in this office. The class leader should understand the life of the congregation as a whole, its collective gifts and graces including those of his/her class members. He/she should know the needs of the community at large. Because the focus of his/her office is discipleship, rather than program or administration, he will be able to bring all of these diverse factors together in mission and ministry. The Biblical model of leadership is built on two concepts: **(1) a servant leads by leading, and (2) a leader leads by serving.** Jesus demonstrated the first principle, that we serve by leading, by taking the risk of calling people to follow Him. He exposed Himself/herself to being misunderstood, criticized, and ridiculed. So the class leader exposes himself to the same situations by taking risks, but the possible consequences of this risk taking more than make up for it. The class leader provides a sense of purpose and vision for the members. He initiates activities which helps members to know each other better. He/she encourages the members to use their spiritual gifts and other resources to serve through their participation in the various activities.

The second concept, leading by serving, was demonstrated by Jesus throughout the Gospels. Jesus served his followers. He not only washed their feet but he calmed them in their storms, taught them in their confusion and prayed for them in their weakness. He fed the thousands, healed the sick, cleansed the lepers, clothed the naked, guided the lost and forgave the sinner. Zacchaeus needed a new start, Nicodemus a new perspective, the woman at the well a new relationship. These were all people with very real needs: each needing to be saved, each being served by Jesus. "I came that they might have Life, and have it more abundantly. I am the good shepherd. The good shepherd lays down his life for the sheep"(John 10:10-11). The class leader who is to lead must be able to perceive the needs and provide the service.

The class leader must be committed to growing in his relationship with Jesus Christ. He/she must be willing to get involved in other people's lives. The leader must be interested in each person in the group. He/she needs to get to know them—by questioning, communicating care and demonstrating spiritual concern. The leader not only must be interested in the group's well being, he/she must be interested in the well being of each individual member as well. A sensitive and caring class leader discerns those needs and creates an environment for growth. The Bible is filled with words which reflect caring— encourage, comfort, exhort, admonish, and teach.

Skills Fundamental To A Class Leader

Leaders are not born. They are developed through work, commitment and love for Jesus Christ. There are some important skills we can develop if we are willing to work on them.

Listening — The Scriptures teach us, "Be quick to hear, slow to speak" **(James 1:19).** Listening is a skill which so often is not practiced; therefore, we do not reap its benefits.

Asking Questions — Many members would like their ideas known but find it difficult to get past that initial barrier of fear. The class leader must acquire the skill of asking non-threatening questions that make persons feel comfortable and draw them out. Ask about their background, hobbies and friends. What do they like to do with leisure time, with holidays?

Communicating care, warmth and reassurance — A smile conveys warmth and is invaluable in making persons feel comfortable. The leader should convey this warmth and caring attitude when making contacts with individual members and also in the class meeting.

Involving Members In Life of Group — Members of the class should be encouraged to take an active part in the life of the group by participating in the class meetings. Unity and bonding of the group can be enhanced early by asking for volunteers to assume certain responsibilities at the class meetings. The leader should not dominate during times of discussions and study. Group participation should be encouraged.

Solving Problems — It has been said that problems are human. As in any group there will be some confusion and disagreement or tension. This happens in any and every human relationship. Often these problems reflect a need for more love or clearer communication or even greater kindness. At other times a difficulty may require more tolerance or some type of compromise or deeper understanding. The leader is in a position to identify a problem and facilitate its constructive resolution. The class leader in these situations will be most helpful by creating an atmosphere that is affirming of people. Jesus on one occasion said, "Blessed are the peacemakers..." **(Matt. 5:9).**

Preparing for the class meeting — Preparing for the class meeting perhaps requires more discipline than skill. The more we do it the more proficient we become. First and foremost, we should pray for God's guidance and the members openness to God's activity. The leader should be familiar with the text to the studied in order to answer relevant questions, and also to pose relevant questions. The class members time is valuable and the leader should know how to use the limited time of the meetings to make the most of it.

Developing and Training Future Leaders — The reproduction of disciples is the primary principle of the mandate of Matthew 28:19-20. It is obvious that leaders are needed to fulfill this mandate. The class system is an ideal and practical structure to identify, nurture, and develop potential leaders. The class leader must constantly ask, "Who in this group has the gifts and graces to develop into a leader of a small group (class leader)." The leader must deliberately encourage members in their spiritual growth, in their personal discipleship, and their identification of spiritual gifts. The class leader must invest in individuals by praying for them and actively helping them develop the character and skills of a disciple. We do all that we can do in ministering to our class, but ultimately it is God and the Holy Spirit that assure the growth. We must always remember that it is God's grace and presence, not ours.

Structuring The Class

In structuring the class system there are several essential issues to be considered: (1) What purpose will the group serve? (2) Who and how many should be included in each group? (3) What should take place in the first meeting? (4) What is the desired size of the group? In an earlier discussion we discussed the different types of small groups. Whatever method is used to structure the class, its purpose and task must be clearly defined. The CME Discipline defines the purpose and task from a fundamental standpoint. The possibilities for ministry may be viewed from a much broader standpoint., This is the rationale for using the term "Small Group Ministry". It is recognized that in our churches there are many models for small group ministry, and it may not be necessary for us to start from the ground floor by "re-inventing the wheel". Small group ministry exists in the various organizations, clubs, auxiliaries and boards. Choirs and usher boards are excellent examples of small groups where persons worship, are nurtured, and discover a sense of community and fellowship. In structuring the class system, it may be possible to organize around the existing small groups. It would certainly afford the opportunity to emphasize discipleship training in addition to its other tasks and purposes for being.

Called To Be A Class Leader

The call to be a class leader comes in two ways: (1) the inward call, and (2) the outward call. Both are important, but it is the inward call which will exert more influence on the person in making the decision to become a class leader.

The inward call from God is often subtle, but it is persistent. Throughout the Bible there are numerous instances when God calls someone to do his work, sometimes subtle and sometimes dramatic. God used a burning bush to get Moses' attention; for Paul it was a blinding light and being knocked off his beast. Both esperiences were quite dramatic. Then, we remember the story of Samuel, and how God called him when he was lying down in the temple. At first he thought it was the priest Eli who was calling him, and three times he arose and went to the old man, only to be told that it was not Eli who had called him. Finally Eli realized it was God who was calling the boy, and told him that the next time he heard the call he should say, "Speak, Lord, for your servant is listening I Sam. 3:2-10).

When we are being called, these urgings will come from various sources. We may receive them at times of meditation, during periods of prayer, or as we read and study the Bible. In worship service it may come through the sermon, singing a hymn, or even during moments of silent meditation. These promptings may come to us through friends who give new insights and assurances. In so many ways the Holy Spirit urges us to recognize the call.

The outward call will come to us in the form of being asked by the pastor to consider the office of class leader. It is likely that you will receive affirmation from fellow church members that will help you to discern the call to this office.

Even after receiving both the **inward call** and **outward call,** one will likely feel insecure or even unworthy to function in this capacity. Earlier we mentioned that there is no perfect leader except Jesus Christ. Each of us are unworthy and limited as human beings, but it is the Holy Spirit that empowers us to do the work of the church. Remember how Jesus took the small amount of fish and loaves the little boy offered. He blessed them and they were multiplied. When we are willing to give whatever gifts and talent, whether they are meager or otherwise, Jesus accepts them, blesses them and then multiplies them. So, accepting the office of class leader merely requires a commitment to Jesus and being willing to accept the grace of God by following the simple teachings of Jesus Christ, growing and being nurtured in discipleship. The Holy Spirit will empower us to do that which we are called to do. In accepting the office we will enjoy the fellowship of other class leaders. A sense of community and bonding will develop. We must engage in constant prayer asking God for guidance and strength as the "tempter" is ever present; "For we wrestle not against flesh and blood, but against principalities, against powers, against the rulers of darkness of this world, against spiritual wickedness in high places" **(Eph. 6:12).**

The Class Leaders' Meeting

After completing the process of appointing potential leaders, a meeting should be scheduled. This meeting will include all leaders and pastoral staff. The session will be conducted on a workshop approach. The purpose for this session is two fold: (1) to present the Biblical basis for the class leader system and (2) to develop goals and objectives of the class leader system.

The agenda for the second meeting of the class leaders will consist of, (1) Organizing the classes, and (2) Assigning class leaders to classes. Most churches have some type of grouping or divisions used for special days or programs. Some of these lists will be most useful in re-aligning and balancing the various classes. There is no hard and fast rule in assigning leaders to the classes. Some pastors will prefer to assign leaders to the classes after the groupings have been made. Other pastors may prefer to do the grouping after the leaders have been assigned. There are advantages and disadvantages to both approaches. In the end, it is just a matter of choice. Experience has shown that it is easier to maintain balance between the classes when the leaders are involved in this process before they are assigned to a class.

When the leaders meet to enter the process of assigning members to the classes there are some guiding principles to be considered. There should be open discussion of factors that most likely will have a direct effect on the makeup of the classes. Some things to be considered are: where people live, age levels, special interests, and even family groupings. This is the time when you may want to take advantage of existing groups within the congregation. Keep in mind as the classes are being formed that they should be as representative as possible of the congregation as a whole. No class should include all of the inactive members, difficult members, and those confined to convalescent homes, etc. These meetings should be approached with an attitude of prayer and openness so that the Holy Spirit will direct, lead and teach as we engage in these activities.

Knowing the members of your class is extremely important and will be a most exciting experience and to some degree, a most baffling experience. Perhaps this is true because human personality will not conform or fit into any preconceived or ordered category.

Whereas each of us has a wide range of acquaintances, our circle of intimate friends are rather limited. It is a fact that each person has an intimate circle of friendships averaging about eight other people. Of course this takes into consideration that some of us are more introverted, and some of us are more extroverted. The results is that we get to know very little about persons with whom we come in contact on a regular basis.

As the class leader gets involved in the process of getting to know the members, it will become apparent how different individuals are and how they react differently under the same situations. It is recognized that members have much in common, such as membership in the same church and somewhat of a common value base; however, they will respond and react quite differently taking into consideration their individual characteristics, of temperaments, interests, habits, beliefs and convictions. David Watson states it quite succinctly in his book on class leaders, "...you are now in the people business. You are discovering what every pastor discovers in his first pastorate; that in creating the human race, God has made no two people alike. Human beings have infinite diversity."

Since there is a crisis at the heart of the church because the church, for the most part, is not making Christian disciples, then it follows that the role of the pastor must change in order to address this crisis and need. To become discipling–making pastors according to D. T. Niles "means not merely a change of direction of soul, that in one more life God's purpose for all is achieved, and through one more life God's will on earth is done." That is to say, the changing of labels or titles that we give to pastors will not help alleviate our critical problems whether we call them reverend, minister or doctor. No, in order to effectively deal with this crisis there must be a change of purpose, attitude, direction and spirit.

We are convinced that the modern role of a discipline making–pastor requires a fresh and different interpretation and application of the Biblical concept of shepherds than is traditionally given. While the role of a shepherd has been portrayed as passive, gentle, nonconfrontational, caring and ready to answer every call of the sheep; the other role of a shepherd should be emphasized and applied to the ministry of pastors. That role is that the shepherd should feed, teach, protect, discipline and lead.

In the contextual usage of Old Testament passages such as **Ezekiel 34:1-31** and **Zechariah 11:4-14** God declared His dissatisfaction for selfish shepherds and His determination to replace them with shepherd that would protect, provide for and effectively lead His sheep. Based upon these passages the discipline, making pastor must do a more effective job of teaching, protecting those who are ready to help lead, providing encouragement and support, and leading congregations.

This new interpretation of the role of a shepherd will help clear up misconceptions about the pastor as the one person to lead the congregation and focus on the pastor as the **chief shepherd** who trains, develops, and empowers, other shepherds to help lead the congregation. The role then of the disciple-making pastor is to train and develop other leaders in such a way which results in team leadership and team management in the local church.

The Broad Perspective of A Disciple-Making Pastor

Too many pastors have a microtheology of the church. They understand and relate to the Church in bits and pieces. When a church is divided up into pieces, they understand the evangelism piece, the Missionary Society piece, the Sunday School piece and etc., but a disciple-making pastor understands the big picture of the Church as one body or organism. As apostle Paul has pointed out in I Cor. 12:25-28, the church has many parts but one body, and all parts (organizations) are inter-related and the actions of each affects the others as well as the whole church.

As a disciple-making pastor sees the big picture of the church as one body, he also sees that it has but one mission which is to make disciples. This led Ronald Miller to proclaim that:

> Mission is not a special function of a part of the church. It is the whole church in action. It is the body of Christ expressing Christ's concern for the whole world. It is God's people seeking to make all persons members of the people of God.

As the disciple-making pastor understands and teaches this broad perspective of what the church is and what its mission is, then each organization or part of the church will grasp that it is not separate from the church and that all parts are to participate in the same mission which is to make disciples. Sunday School teachers will understand that their task is to do more than have students memorize a few passages of Scripture, read a Sunday School book and appear in the Easter and Christmas programs—their task is to make Christian disciples. Missionary Society members will understand that their task is more than marching in white dresses— as beautiful as they look — providing food and clothing for the poor and reporting on how many they helped—their task is to make Christian Disciples, and stewards and stewardesses will understand that their task is more than collecting, paying and counting money or attending church conferences to help determine how money will be spent— their task also is to make Christian disciples.

This broad perspective of the church and its mission will cause disciple-making pastors and church members to perceive new opportunities, new plans and a new vision for the church because they will have seen God's vision for the world.

The Commitment Of A Disciple-Making Pastor

According to Bill Hull, the disciple-making pastor has at least four basic commitments:

> He is committed to placing disciple making at the heart of the church. He commits himself to the clear identification and communication of the roles of the pastor, the people, and the discipling process. He is committed to the priesthood of all believers, and He has a commitment to multiplication.

We agree with Dr. Hull that these commitments are necessary because when a pastor is committed in the areas mentioned, that pastor will place disciple-making at the center of the church, proclaim discipleship from the pulpit, model disciple-making as a part of his administrative style and include discipleship as a part of his relationship with members of the church.

This commitment to disciple-making must grow out of a commitment to Jesus Christ. For so long we as pastors and leaders have tried leading God's church our way. Therefore, a commitment to discipleship requires complete commitment of ourselves, body and soul, time and talent to Jesus Christ. As we become committed to Jesus, then we are willing to discard our methods and accept His method, submit our pride and power, surrender our egos about who will get the credit and let Jesus receive the praise and glory. And yet, the disciple making-pastor should be aware that as the church he/she is serving starts multiplying and penetrating the world, some recognition and credit will be given to him/her.

Thus the main motive for committing one's self to becoming a disciple-making pastor must grow out of love for Christ and love for His church. Love for Christ for what He has done for us is the deepest ingredient in the motivation to discipleship. "We love, because He first loved us **(I John 4:19).** To know that we are loved by Christ reaches deeper into our lives than anything else can. For this love is wholly undeserved. Others may love us because they see something lovely in us. However, as disciples our love for Christ is based upon an awareness and appreciation for His love which motivates us to train, teach and develop others who can be very unloving at times.

The Practice of A Disciple-Making Pastor

While various writers such as Lyle Schaller, Howard Hendrick and Bill Hull have listed a number of practices that the disciple-making pastor should adhere to, we wish to reduce them to what we believe are the three most essential practices of the disciple-making pastor: (1) Effectively uses the small group for disciple–making; (2) Practices sound principles for selecting leaders; and (3) believes in and practices the usage of lay ministers for carrying out ministries of the church.

1. Effectively uses the small group for disciple-making.

Disciple-making exists in three primary forms: The large group, the small group, and one on one. The primary tool of the large group is to address the public through music, film, drama and the spoken word. However, it lacks the personal touch, depth and fine tuning that is necessary to complete the process of making disciples. It is an important step, but is only a start.

One on one provides a great deal of fine-tuning, but it takes too long and is an insufficient use of a person's time. One on one is important to the process, but becomes a problem when it is considered as the primary method. One on one as a primary method for disciple-making leads to a waste of time and resources.

Jesus demonstrated the superiority of the small group for training. Even though Jesus taught the multitude, fed five thousand and preached the sermon on the Mount to a large crowd, Jesus chose the small group of twelve for the intensive training to become his disciples.

While the large group is used for inspiration and motivation concerning the work, the small group should be used to take them to another level. Bill Hull states that "if the large group interest people by telling them what and why, the small group trains them by showing them how and doing it with them." And Hull reminds us that "Jesus waited until the twelve were well established before He chose them to be with Him, and He spent five months of further training before he commissioned them to ministry".

Jesus saw the need to employ the method of training small groups in order to make them disciples. The CME Church has mostly abandoned this process. Historically, the CME Church not only had class leaders but this small group of Christian leaders was well trained and met weekly to report the funds they had collected as well as to participate in an intensive group learning process. This leads me to the conviction that disciple–making pastors must lead churches back to the process of intensive training, developing and commissioning class leaders. Also, this process must be supplemented by starting and training other discipleship groups within the church.

2. Practices sound principles for selecting leaders

While the previous topic focused on training church members in small groups before they are commissioned to go make disciples, it should be pointed out that pastors and members in our church have too often made the tragic mistake of putting people in key positions who had not been taught, and many of them are not teachable.

This raises the question as to whether we are using sound principles for selecting leaders such as stewards, stewardesses, trustees and class leaders? An obvious answer to the question is no. But if God saw the need to carefully select people such as Noah to build the Ark, Abraham to be the seed of the chose people, David to unite the Israelite nation and the apostle Paul to carry the gospel to the gentiles, we in the CME Church also need to utilize sound principles for selecting leaders.

Sound principles for selecting leaders should be based on the qualifications that are grounded in the Bible. These include those referred to in **Luke 16:10, II Tim. 2:2, I Tim. 3:1-10 and Titus 1:5-9.** These selection principles also should include the elevation of those who go through the process of being trained.

As Jesus required His disciples to be trained before they were commissioned to go make disciples, this writer is strongly advocating that pastors ensure that lay members are well trained before they are recommended for such positions as stewards, stewardesses, trustees, class leaders, directors of Christian Education and other leading positions in the church.

In fact, if the CME Church is ready to take seriously the making of disciples, we must include in our 1994 General Conference legislation a requirement for the laity to complete a course of study on discipleship before they can be confirmed as officers in the church.

3. Believes in and practices the usage of lay ministers for carrying out ministries of the church.

One of the harmful and self defeating practices of pastors, along with the high expectations and persuasion of church members, is that pastors are trying to do too many things for too many people at too many different times. This is a serious problem in the CME Church where churches expect pastors to be jacks-of-all-trades, a vocation at which they are failing. What is even worse is that many pastors believe that they are supposed to be jacks-of-all-trades and are therefore, trying in vain to prove they can be. Their lives become a series of rabbit trails that take them in circles and off course, and as a result, pastors are being very busy going down many trails and accomplishing very little for the Lord.

We wish to caution pastors and the CME Church that requiring or expecting pastors to be jacks-of-all-trades is not Biblical and therefore is not Christian.

The Bible in such Scriptures as Epheasian 4:11 points out that each Christian is given a spiritual gift or some gifts, but no Christian is given all the gifts for leading God's Church. When properly applied, this Scripture clearly indicates that regardless of what school or seminary a pastor attended, the academic excellence or acquired abilities he attained, no pastor or church leader has been gifted by God to be a jack-of-all-trades or lead every ministry in the church.

This led Bill Hull to accurately state that the proper use or role of the pastor is as follows: "The pastor's work is to declare the what and why of ministry, then to train all willing members to do that work. After that, he must manage the ministry. Declare, train and manage: That is the commissioned work of the pastor".

There is a desperate need then for pastors to train lay

persons and use them to lead various ministries of the church. Remembering that while some pastors are gifted and trained for counseling, it is not Biblical that pastors should do all the counseling, all the hospital visiting, all the consoling of bereaved, etc. The training and using of lay people to lead various ministries in the church would lead to the development of para-professional lay people who could effectively lead and help develop such ministries as a Christian counseling ministry, hospital visitation ministry, grief ministry, feeding ministry, prison ministry, infant nursery ministry, singles ministry, married couples ministry or whatever ministry that meets the need of the people of that church and community.

We are convinced that proper training and utilizing of lay people in leading various ministries of the CME Church will lead to renewed enthusiasm, vigor and excitement in our churches and at the same time enable us to more effectively meet the needs of our communities and usher in a new day of church growth.

Conclusion

As God's people called Christian Methodists, we have a ministry to carry out — both individually and corporately; we have a mission to perform. Jesus did not leave us with vague ideas about what we are to do. Instead, He gave us specific instructions on how to accomplish our mission. While He was on earth, He gathered His disciples together and gave them a vision of what His church is to accomplish. He gave the church a mission. Jesus presents that mission in **Matthew 28:19-20,** which is what we call the "Great Commission."

> Go, ye therefore and make disciples of all the nations, baptizing them in the name of the Father, and the Son, and the Holy Spirit, teaching them to observe all things, whatsoever I have commanded you; and lo, I am with you always, even to the end of the age.

In the Great Commission, Jesus presents disciple-making as the goal and mission of church ministry. The church is to make disciples who will be obedient to the task and mission of living in the world and touching every aspect of life with God's image and presence. Why is it so important for the church to make disciples? Disciples are people who have committed themselves to living totally under the Lordship of Christ in every aspect of life. They are spiritual people. They are the ones—the only ones—who can make the spiritual impact God desires in the world.

Jesus' instruction for the church is to make and teach disciples. God has assigned the preacher/pastor/teacher to teach His people. The task of the pastor/teacher is to inform and inspire God's people to do His work. Otherwise, there is the possibility that God's people will get used to enjoying the blessings and neglect their job of going and making disciples. The pastor does not need to go looking for a program, a mission, or a focus, it has already been given — **"to make disciples."**

After all has been said about making and equipping disciples, and carrying out the mission of the Church, we must be reminded that the task is impossible from the human standpoint. If the task of the church is to make disciples, it is humanly impossible to fulfill this role by our strength alone. Where shall the power come from to facilitate our task? It is only through the presence of the resurrected Saviour, living and reigning in his church, that the task can be faced and carried out. We have the assurance of His claim and authority: "All power in heaven and earth has been given unto me." He has empowered and delegated that authority to his disciples. And since this is true, then the pastors and the church can go forth to make disciples with the greatest power in the universe in them.

Finally, we also have His own words that we have all the help we need. In John 15:7-8, He instructs us: "If ye abide in me, and my words abide in you, ye shall ask what ye will, and it shall be done unto you. Herein is my Father glorified, that ye bear much fruit; so shall ye be my disciples." We are told in Matthew 28:20 that He will never leave us nor forsake us: "Lo, I am with you always, even unto the end of the world." If pastors go forth to equip and make disciples without His presence, they are doomed, "for without me ye can do nothing" (John 15:5b). If they go at His command and with His power, they shall conquer all obstacles and realize anew the blessings of the early church in Acts 2:47, "And the Lord was adding to their number day by day those who were being saved." Yes! the dry bones will live again in spite of the rumor that they are dead.

**"To Him be glory, in Christ Jesus,
Throughout all ages, world without
end; Amen!" (Ephesians 2:14-18)**

REFERENCES

Casgrove, Jr., Francis M. *Essentials of Discipleship*
Colorado Springs: Navpress, 1985

Hendrick, Howard, Speech At "Disciple Making in the
Eighties Conference." October, 1983

Hendricksen, Walter A. *Disciples are Made Not Born.*
Wheaton: Victor Books, 1988

Hull, Bill, *The Disciple Making Pastor.*
Tarrytown, NY: Fleming H. Revell Com., 1988

Kuhne, Gary W. *The Dynamics of Discipleship Training —
Being and Producing Spiritual Leaders.*
Grand Rapids: Zondervan, 1982

Miller, Donald G. *The Nature and Mission of the Church.*
Richmond, CA: John Knox Press, 1957

Moore, Waylon B. *Multiplying Disciples.*
Colorado Springs: Navpress, 1991

Niles, D.T. *That They Might Have Life.*
New York: Harper and Brothers Publishers, 1951

Shenk, David W. and Stutzman, Ervin R.
Creating Communities of the Kingdom.
Scottsdale, PA: Herald Press, 1988

Townsend, Jim. *New Testament Highlights.*
Elgin: David C. Cook, 1988

Trueblood, Elton. *The Best of Elton Trueblood: An
Anthology.* Nashville, TN: Impact Books, 1979

Wagner, Peter C. *Your Spiritual Gifts Can Help Your
Church Grow.*
Ventura, CA Regal Books, 1979